Advancing Islāmic Psychology Education

This book provides academic and clinical institutions for developing their educational programmes in psychology, psychotherapy and counselling from an Islāmic paradigm.

Examining the educational approach in the decolonisation of psychology curricula, the book proposes a vertically and horizontally integrated, embedded curriculum model. This model meets the changing needs of practitioners, incorporating indigenous cultural aspects and emerging technologies to reflect new and creative ways of thinking about delivering education in the post-Covid-19 era. The chapters also demonstrate how curriculum development, based on the principles of Islāmic education, helps institutions to establish purpose, define activities and guide decision-making in educational development. A series of steps for implementing this need-driven educational programme has been suggested.

This practical, concise and evidenced-based text will be a key resource for educators and trainers. It will help them understand how to redesign or suggest changes to curriculum structure, shape and content in Islāmic psychology, psychotherapy and counselling for undergraduate, postgraduate and continuing professional development levels of education.

G. Hussein Rassool, PhD, is a professor of Islāmic psychology and an Islāmic psychotherapist. He is involved in the development of Islāmic psychology and psychotherapy as a discipline and is a pioneer in the theoretical and conceptual development of Islāmic psychology education. He is a consultant at the Department of Psychology at Riphah International University, the chair of Al-Balkhi's Institute of Research and Education and a director of studies at the Department of Islamic Psychology, Psychotherapy & Counselling, Al Balagh Academy.

Focus Series on Islāmic Psychology
Series Editor: Professor Dr. G. Hussein Rassool,
Professor of Islāmic Psychology

About the Series

In contemporary times, there is increasing focus on the need to adapt approaches of psychology, counselling psychology and psychotherapy to accommodate the integration of spirituality and psychology. With the increasing focus on the need to meet the wholistic needs of Muslims, there was a call to adapt approaches to the understanding of behaviour and experiences from an Islāmic epistemological and ontological worldview.

The aim of the Focus Series on Islāmic psychology and psychotherapy is to introduce a range of educational, clinical and research interventions relating to Islāmic psychology and psychotherapy that are authentic, practical, concise, and based on cutting-edge research. Each volume focuses on a particular aspect of Islāmic psychology and psychotherapy, its application with a specific client group, a particular methodology or approach, or a critical analysis of existing and emergent theoretical and historical ideas.

Each book in the Focus Series is written, in accessible language, with the assumption that the readers have no prior knowledge of Islāmic psychology and psychotherapy.

Advancing Islāmic Psychology Education
Knowledge Integration, Model, and Application
G. Hussein Rassool

Advancing Islāmic Psychology Education
Knowledge Integration, Model, and Application

G. Hussein Rassool

LONDON AND NEW YORK

First published 2023
by Routledge
4 Park Square, Milton Park, Abingdon, Oxon OX14 4RN

and by Routledge
605 Third Avenue, New York, NY 10158

Routledge is an imprint of the Taylor & Francis Group, an informa business

© 2023 G. Hussein Rassool

The right of G. Hussein Rassool to be identified as author of this work has been asserted in accordance with sections 77 and 78 of the Copyright, Designs and Patents Act 1988.

All rights reserved. No part of this book may be reprinted or reproduced or utilised in any form or by any electronic, mechanical, or other means, now known or hereafter invented, including photocopying and recording, or in any information storage or retrieval system, without permission in writing from the publishers.

Trademark notice: Product or corporate names may be trademarks or registered trademarks, and are used only for identification and explanation without intent to infringe.

British Library Cataloguing-in-Publication Data
A catalogue record for this book is available from the British Library

Library of Congress Cataloging-in-Publication Data
Names: Rassool, G. Hussein, author.
Title: Advancing Islamic psychology education : knowledge integration, model, and application / G. Hussein Rassool.
Description: Abingdon, Oxon ; New York, NY : Routledge, 2024. | Series: Focus series on Islamic psychology | Includes bibliographical references and index.
Identifiers: LCCN 2023014937 (print) | LCCN 2023014938 (ebook) | ISBN 9781032359731 (hardback) | ISBN 9781032359724 (paperback) | ISBN 9781003329596 (ebook)
Subjects: LCSH: Islam—Psychology. | Psychology—Religious aspects—Islam. | Psychology—Study and teaching—Islamic countries. | Education—Islamic countries.
Classification: LCC BP175 .R374 2024 (print) | LCC BP175 (ebook) | DDC 297.2/615—dc23/eng/20230414
LC record available at https://lccn.loc.gov/2023014937
LC ebook record available at https://lccn.loc.gov/2023014938

ISBN: 978-1-032-35973-1 (hbk)
ISBN: 978-1-032-35972-4 (pbk)
ISBN: 978-1-003-32959-6 (ebk)

DOI: 10.4324/9781003329596

Typeset in Times New Roman
by Apex CoVantage, LLC

Dedicated to Idrees Khattab ibn Adam Ibn Hussein ibn Hassim Ibn Sahaduth Ibn Rosool Ibn Olee Al Mauritiusy, Isra Oya, Asiyah Maryam, Idrees Khattab, Adam Ali Hussein, Reshad Hassan, Yasmin Soraya, BeeBee Mariam, Bibi Safian and Hassim, Dr Najmul Hussein and Mohammed Ali.

Abu Hurayrah reported the Prophet Muhammad ﷺ as saying: *"If anyone pursues a path in search of knowledge, Allāh will thereby make easy for him a path to paradise; and he who is made slow by his actions will not be speeded by his genealogy"* (Sunan Abu Dâwud).

Contents

List of figures	x
List of tables	xi
Preface	xii
Acknowledgements	xiv

1 Shifting the paradigm: decolonising psychology knowledge   1

2 Principles of Islāmic psychology education   23

3 Islāmisation of knowledge and knowledge integration   36

4 Curriculum design and development   47

5 Readiness for knowledge integration of Islāmic ethics and Islāmic psychology: an integrated research study   61

6 Models and process of curriculum integration and knowledge integration   84

7 Rassool's vertical and horizontal integrated embedded curriculum model of Islāmic psychology   99

8 Course scheme in Islāmic psychology: knowledge integration   107

Index   *125*

Figures

1.1	Classification of the term *'ilm* in the Islāmic tradition	3
1.2	Sources of knowledge	5
1.3	A simple model of Islāmic psychology	16
4.1	A map of curriculum design and development	48
4.2	Product and process models	50
4.3	Constructive alignment	57
5.1	Model of knowledge integration	63
6.1	Knowledge integration	84
6.2	Knowledge integration mechanisms	91
6.3	Rassool's process-driven model of knowledge integration for the psychology curriculum	93
7.1	Rassool's framework for Islāmisation of knowledge	100
7.2	Berghout's model of Islāmisation	101
7.3	Rassool's proposed educational conceptual framework for knowledge integration in psychology based on the *Tawhîd* paradigm	102
7.4	Rassool's vertical and horizontal integration curriculum approach	103

Tables

1.1	Paradigm of Islāmic psychology	9
1.2	Limitations of secular psychology	11
2.1	Al-Ghazâlî's code of ethics for students	28
4.1	Coherence in curriculum organisation	55
5.1	Reliability of scales, mean, standard deviation and skewness (N = 41)	68
5.2	Demographic profile of the sample (N = 41)	70
5.3	Frequency and percentage (high and low values), mean and standard deviation of the level of Islāmic moral values of lecturers (N = 41)	70
5.4	Perceptions of knowledge integration and attitude towards knowledge integration	71
5.5	Study variables of role behaviours	72
5.6	ANOVA: summary of selected variables	72
5.7	Correlation between Islāmic moral values, perception of knowledge integration and attitude towards knowledge integration in university lecturers (N = 41)	72
5.8	Regression coefficients of Islāmic moral values, perception of knowledge integration and attitude towards knowledge integration	73
5.9	Regression coefficients of Islāmic moral values, perception of knowledge integration and attitude towards knowledge integration	73
5.10	Regression coefficients of Islāmic moral values, perception of knowledge integration and attitude towards knowledge integration	73
6.1	Fogarty's model in the design of curriculum integration	86
6.2	Harden's 11 steps on the integration ladder	87

Preface

During the past four decades, there has been a reawakening of Islāmic psychology and appearance, albeit limited, of a growth in the literature on Islāmic psychology and psychotherapy. With the increasing focus on the need to meet the holistic needs of Muslims and to adapt approaches to the understanding of behaviour and experiences from an Islāmic perspective, the books from the Focus Series on Islamic Psychology are short, practical, concise, no-nonsense and evidenced-based literature on Islāmic psychology and psychotherapy. This series of books examine psychology, psychotherapy and counselling from an Islāmic paradigm and its applications in education and clinical practice.

With the proliferation of courses, formal and informal, in Islāmic psychology, psychotherapy and counselling at undergraduate, postgraduate and continuing professional development levels, there is an increasing need to offer a conceptual framework to those responsible for educational and curriculum development. This book is part of the Focus Series on Islāmic Psychology that explores educational and curriculum development from an Islāmic paradigm. It examines the educational approach in the decolonisation of psychology curricula and proposes a conceptual framework: a vertically and horizontally integrated, embedded curriculum model. There is a need to adapt educational and training programmes to meet the changing needs of practitioners, to incorporate indigenous cultural aspects and emerging technologies and to reflect on creative ways of thinking about delivering education in the post-Covid-19 era.

The contents of the book also demonstrate how curriculum development, based on the principles of Islāmic education, helps institutions to establish purpose, define activities, and guide decision-making in educational development. The purpose of the book is to provide some general instructions to academic and clinical institutions to develop or revise their educational programmes in Islāmic psychology, psychotherapy and counselling and suggests a series of steps to follow in creating need-driven educational programmes.

There is a dearth of relevant literature on curriculum development in Islāmic psychology, psychotherapy and counselling and suitable handbooks that cover the proposed content of the book. Currently, most texts on Islāmic psychology do not cover the nature and content of the proposed book. The book is, at least in part, a response to the questions posed by researchers, academics and clinicians, concerning the nature and focus of educational programmes in this field of knowledge. This book makes a pioneering contribution to the integration of the Islāmic sciences in the curriculum of educational programmes in psychology, psychotherapy and counselling. It will be a key resource for those responsible as educators and trainers to understand how to integrate knowledge and redesign or make changes to curriculum structure, shape and content in Islāmic psychology.

Acknowledgements

All praise is due to Allāh and may the peace and blessings of Allāh be upon our Prophet Muhammad ﷺ, his family and his companions.

I would like to thank Grace McDonnell at Routledge for her valuable and constructive suggestions during the development of the proposal and during the process of writing, as well as Sarah Hafeez for general support. It is with immense gratitude that I acknowledge my learning from colleagues from the Centre for Islāmic Psychology (CIP) and the Department of Psychology, Riphah International University, and students from the Department of Psychology, International Open University, where I developed the undergraduate course in Islāmic psychology.

I am thankful to my beloved parents, who taught me the value of education. I owe my gratitude to Mariam, Idrees Khattab Ibn Adam Ali Hussein Ibn Hussein Ibn Hassim Ibn Sahaduth Ibn Rosool Al Mauritiusy, Adam Ali Hussein, Reshad Hasan, Yasmin Soraya, Isra Oya, Asiyah Maryam, Nabila Akhrif, Nusaybah Burke, Musa Burke, Dr Najmul Hussein, and Mohammed Ali for their unconditional love and who provided unending inspiration.

I would like to acknowledge the contributions my teachers who enabled me, through my own reflective practices, to understand authentic Islām and, from their guidance, to follow the right path of the creed of *Ahlus-Sunnah wa'l-Jama'ah*. Finally, whatever benefits and correctness you find within this book are out of the grace of Allāh alone, and whatever mistakes you find are mine alone. I pray to Allāh to forgive me for any unintentional shortcomings regarding the contents of this book and to make this humble effort helpful and fruitful to any interested parties.

Whatever of good befalls you, it is from Allāh; and whatever of ill befalls you, it is from yourself.

(An-Nisā' [The Women] 4:79)

Acknowledgements xv

Praise be to Allāh, we seek His help and His forgiveness. We seek refuge with Allāh from the evil of our own souls and from our bad deeds. Whomsoever Allāh guides will never be led astray, and whomsoever Allāh leaves astray, no one can guide. I bear witness that there is no god but Allāh, and I bear witness that Muhammad is His slave and Messenger (*Sunan al-Nasa'i: Kitaab al-Jumu'ah, Baab kayfiyyah al-khutbah*).

- *Fear Allāh as He should be feared and die not except in a state of Islām (as Muslims) with complete submission to Allāh* (Ali-'Imran 3:102).[1]
- *O mankind! Be dutiful to your Lord, Who created you from a single person, and from him He created his wife, and from them both He created many men and women, and fear Allāh through Whom you demand your mutual (rights), and (do not cut the relations of) the wombs (kinship) Surely, Allāh is Ever an All-Watcher over you)* (Al-Nisā' 4:1).
- *O you who believe! Keep your duty to Allāh and fear Him and speak (always) the truth)* (Al-Aĥzāb 33:70).
- *What comes to you of good is from Allāh, but what comes to you of evil, [O man], is from yourself* (An-Nisā 4:79).

The essence of this book is based on the following notions:

- The fundamental of Islām as a religion is based on the oneness of God.
- The source of knowledge is based on the Qur'ān and Hadith (*Ahl as-Sunnah wa'l-Jamā'ah*).
- Empirical knowledge from sense perception is also a source of knowledge through the work of classical and contemporary Islāmic scholars and research.
- Islām takes a holistic approach to health: physical, psychological, social, emotional, and spiritual health cannot be separated.
- Muslims have a different worldview or perception of illness and health behaviour.
- There is a wide consensus amongst Muslim scholars that psychiatric or psychological disorders are legitimate medical or psychiatric conditions that is distinct from illnesses of a supernatural nature.
- Muslims believe that cures come solely from Allāh (God), but seeking treatment for psychological and spiritual health does not conflict with seeking help from Allāh.

It is a sign of respect that Muslims would utter or repeat the words "Peace and Blessing Be Upon Him" after hearing (or writing) the name of the Prophet Muhammad ﷺ.

Note

1 The translations of the meanings of the verses of the Qur'ān in this book have been taken, with some changes, from Saheeh International, The Qur'ān: Arabic Text with corresponding English meanings.

1 Shifting the paradigm

Decolonising psychology knowledge

Introduction

In contemporary times, the needs to decolonise psychological knowledge as a discipline and psychology as a profession are beyond dispute. Subsequently, Western psychology, with its sub-disciplines and clinical branches, has "for so long dominated the production of theoretical psychological knowledge and therapeutic intervention, and its imposition is reflected in the curriculum contents of psychology programmes, textbooks and clinical applications of tests and other psychosocial interventions" (Rassool, 2021, p. 583). The main schools of thought in psychology were influenced and primed by mostly rationalists, who are mainly atheists or agnostics. The rationalist approach, based on reason and evidence, was overtly antagonistic to religion and spirituality, and created a deep fissure between divine revelation and rationality as sources of knowledge. The absence and scarcity of religion and spirituality visibility in the psychology curriculum remains a significant barrier. The most significant conundrum in psychology departments in Muslim-majority countries is the Eurocentric orientation of psychology curricula and pedagogy in both undergraduate and postgraduate educational programmes, thus teaching "Whiteness" psychology (Williams, 2020). Dudgeon and Walker (2015) suggests, "Psychology colonises both directly through the imposition of universalising, individualistic constructions of human behaviour and indirectly through the negation" (p. 276).

This monocultural approach to psychology knowledge seems problematic for students graduating in psychology in both Western universities and universities in Muslim countries. Students of psychology are being presented with a deficit view of a "soulless" and "Whiteness" psychology without knowledge integration of knowledge diversity, religion and spirituality. This absence prevents students to understand the relationship between spirituality psychological and spiritual health. In effect, students of psychology are failing to understand the effects of colonisation on their psychological knowledge. Due the diversity of population in many countries on the global scale, graduates of psychology or clinical psychologists are encountering a diversity

DOI: 10.4324/9781003329596-1

2 Shifting the paradigm

of patients during clinical practice but lack the cultural competence to meet their bio-psychosocial needs, across socio-cultural context, and those patients who are faith-based. This has consequences for Muslim patients receiving psychological-oriented approaches based on Judeo-Christian values, which are aligned with Western philosophical traditions, social values and agendas (Rose, 1998).

Since the late 20th century, the "Islāmisation of knowledge" movement has primed Muslim scholars and psychologists to reflect on embracing knowledge integration (Islāmic ethics with empirical psychology) and to decolonise psychological knowledge. There has been a paradigm shift for an Islāmic psychology, and this has gone from slowly gathering momentum in the 1980s to becoming a movement today (Waheed & Skinner, 2022). In this context, psychology knowledge must be deconstructed and remodelled to incorporate spirituality and religion. For psychology, the process of decolonisation has begun, and efforts are being made to reconstruct psychology based on an Islāmic epistemological paradigm (Rassool, 2021).

However, there is a dearth of an educational conceptual framework for integrating Islāmic psychology in the literature despite the burgeoning of courses in Islāmic psychology and counselling in the UK, the USA, Australia, Turkey, Pakistan, Malaysia and Indonesia. The aims of this chapter are to examine the dominance of Western paradigm in psychology and the need to decolonise psychology knowledge, and to integrate Islāmic epistemology in empirical psychology disciplines.

Sources of knowledge and knowledge integration

Before moving to the approach and process of decolonisation of psychology knowledge, it would be valuable to briefly examine the sources of knowledge and knowledge integration from an Islāmic perspective. In Arabic language, knowledge is elated to the concept of *'ilm*. However, it is argued that

> [k]nowledge falls short of expressing all the factual and emotional contents of *'ilm*. For *'ilm* is one of those concepts that have dominated Islām and given Muslim civilization its distinctive shape and complexion. In fact, there is no other concept that has been operative as a determinant of Muslim civilization in all its aspects to the same extent as *'ilm*.
>
> (Rosenthal, 2007, pp. 2–3)

In the Islāmic traditions, the term *'ilm* covers all types of knowledge derived from the works of Ibn Sab'in (d. 1270 CE), Al-Āmidī (d. 1233), Abu Hamid Al-Ghazali (d.1111) and Imam Al-Haramayn Al-Juwayni (d. 1083) (see Figure 1.1). The literature from these classical scholars indicate that knowledge is a process of knowing; cognition (*ma'rifah*); obtaining (*idrāk, huṣūl*) or "finding" through mental perception; clarification, assertion and decision

Shifting the paradigm 3

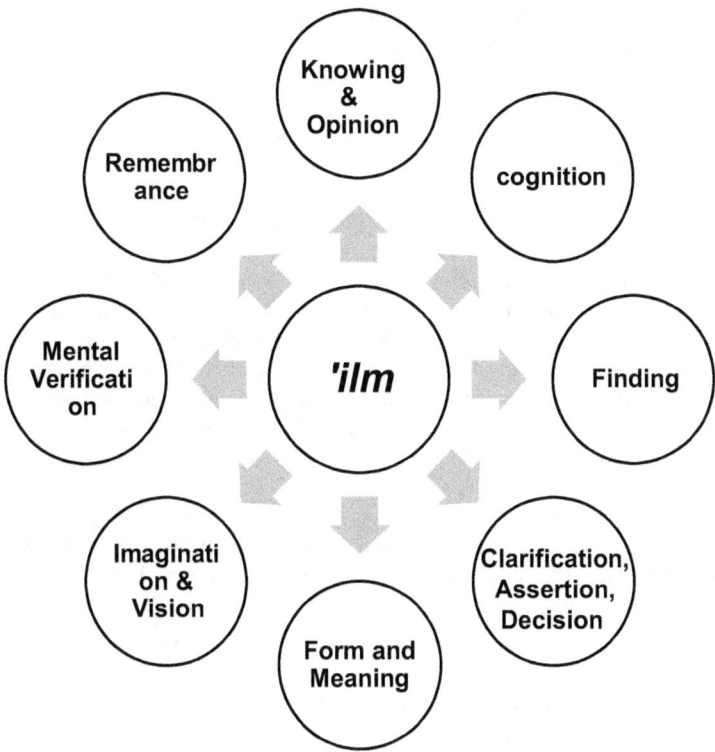

Figure 1.1 Classification of the term *'ilm* in the Islāmic tradition
Source: Adapted from Rosenthal (2007)

(*bayyana, mayyaza, athbata, qaṭa'a*); a form (*ṣūrah*), a concept or meaning (*ma'ana*), a process of mental formation and imagination (*taṣawwur*) and/ or mental verification (*taṣdīq*); belief; remembrance (*dhikr*); imagination (*khayal*), an image, a vision (*ru'ya*), or opinion (*ra'yi*); a motion (*harakah*); and so on (Rosenthal, 2007).

Islām is a religion based on knowledge or the acquisition of knowledge (*'ilm*). This is reflected in the following verses of the Qur'ān:

ٱقْرَأْ بِٱسْمِ رَبِّكَ ٱلَّذِى خَلَقَ
خَلَقَ ٱلْإِنسَٰنَ مِنْ عَلَقٍ
ٱقْرَأْ وَرَبُّكَ ٱلْأَكْرَمُ
ٱلَّذِى عَلَّمَ بِٱلْقَلَمِ
عَلَّمَ ٱلْإِنسَٰنَ مَا لَمْ يَعْلَمْ

4 Shifting the paradigm

- *Read! In the Name of your Lord Who created.*
- *Created man from a clinging substance.*
- *Recite! And your Lord is the Most Generous.*
- *Who taught by the pen.*
- *Taught man that which he knew not.* (*Al-'Alaq* 96:1–5, interpretation of the meaning)

These verses according to the exegesis of Ibn Kathir (2000)

> inform of the beginning of man's creation from a dangling clot, and He taught man that which he did not know. Thus, Allah exalted him and honoured him by giving him knowledge, and it is the dignity that the Father of Humanity, Adam, was distinguished with over the angels. Knowledge sometimes is in the mind, sometimes on the tongue, and sometimes in writing with the fingers. Thus, it may be intellectual, spoken and written. And while the last (written) necessitates the first two (intellectual and spoken), the reverse is not true.

There is persistent emphasis in the Qur'ān, on the importance and significance of knowledge. Allāh commanded His Messenger ﷺ and said:

وَقُل رَّبِّ زِدْنِى عِلْمًا

- *And say*: "*My Lord! Increase me in knowledge.*" (Ta-Ha 20:114, interpretation of the meaning)

Islām calls us to seek knowledge (*'ilm*), and all kinds of beneficial knowledge. This does not only relate to "God's laws and religious injunctions, but also on the importance of seeing, contemplating, and reasoning about the world's creation and its diverse phenomena" (WiseInstitute, 2018). The Messenger of Allāh ﷺ made seeking knowledge an obligation upon every Muslim, and he explained, "The superiority of the scholar over the worshiper is like my superiority over the least of you" (Tirmidhi). The Messenger of Allāh ﷺ said that seeking knowledge is a way to paradise. It was narrated that Abu Hurairah said, "The Messenger of Allah ﷺ said: 'Whoever follows a path in pursuit of knowledge, Allah will make easy for him a path to paradise'" (Ibn Majah). Thus, knowledge has been at the centre of the Islāmic civilisation and paradigm from the outset.

The Qur'ān recognises multiple sources of knowledge amongst which the following are particularly important: revelation, intuition, sense perception and rationality (see Figure 1.2). The primary source of knowledge in Islām is from the Qur'ān and *Sunnah* (*Ilm Naqli*), and secondary source is from rational knowledge based on human intellect (*Aql*), observation and empiricism (*Ilm Aqli*). Divine revelation is the foundation upon which all knowledge is built, being perfect and complete. It has been suggested that the knowledge foundation of the Qur'ān

> is viewed as the springhead of all knowledge and all sciences, not because it contains the knowledge itself but, rather, because it inspires the Muslim to develop a distinctive vision of the unity among the various spheres of knowledge. The notion of this unity arises out of an awareness of the unity of the Divine and its applications to the various spheres of human knowledge.
>
> (Malkawi, 2014, p. 20)

Thus, the Qur'ān becomes one of the primary sources of knowledge and holds supreme to all other sources of knowledge because the contexts are made for all humankind. This is echoed in the following verses of the Qur'ān:

ذَٰلِكَ ٱلْكِتَٰبُ لَا رَيْبَ ۛ فِيهِ ۛ هُدًى لِّلْمُتَّقِينَ

- *This is the Book about which there is no doubt, a guidance of those conscious of God.* (*Taqwa*) (Al-Baqarah 2:2, interpretation of the meaning)

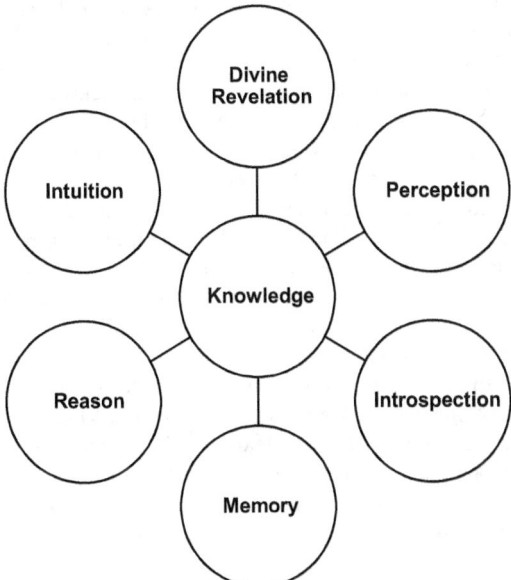

Figure 1.2 Sources of knowledge

6 Shifting the paradigm

There are many types of knowledge in the Qur'ān including knowledge of revelation, the unseen, acquired knowledge, scientific knowledge, intuition and inspiration, Utz (2011) suggests,

> It is only through revelation that we can comprehend the true nature of the soul and the unseen world and ascertain the methods for purifying the soul and developing it to its fullest potential. Allāh is the only One with authentic and complete knowledge of the unseen world, so we turn only to Him for this understanding. Human beings, especially Muslims, must not speculate or guess in relation to this domain.
>
> (p. 39–40)

In addition to the primary source of knowledge from the Qur'ān, there is also the *Hādīth* (refers to the actions, statements, or tacit approvals of the Prophet Muhammad ﷺ). These become the primary and most fundamental sources of knowledge in Islām. From a practical implication of Islām, the Sunnah (refers to the sayings and practices of the Prophet Muhammad ﷺ) is also a source of knowledge for Muslims.

Islāmisation of knowledge: knowledge integration

It is the Islāmic awakening (*aṣ-Ṣaḥwah l-'Islāmiyyah*), motivated by a desire to return to the fundamental of Islāmic teaching and practices based on the Qur'ān and Sunnah, that primed the way for the Islāmisation of knowledge. Rassool (2021) suggested that the emergence, current conceptualisations and the status of Islāmic psychology should be viewed in their broader context – namely, the Islāmisation of knowledge (IOK) movement. According to Ragab (1999), Islāmisation refers to the "Integration of Islāmic revealed knowledge and the human sciences." The IOK movement gained momentum in the 1970s "with the rise of the plight of the Muslim *Ummah*, the secularisation the educational system in Muslim majority countries, the global re-awakening of Islāmic consciousness, and the concern of Muslim scholars towards the adoption of Western-oriented values and life-styles by Muslims" (Rassool, 2022, p. 14), as well as the incompatibility of a reductionist, scientific, naturalist and secular traditions in contemporary psychology. Academic institutions, including the International Islāmic University of Malaysia, and the emerging publications from the International Institute of Islāmic Thought paved the way to Islāmise the social sciences, including the discipline of psychology.

Knowledge in the Islāmic traditions is based on holism. That is nature and process of knowledge focuses on

> integration, rather than separation, inclusiveness, rather than contraction, harmony, rather than dichotomy, cooperation, rather than conflict, comprehensive excellence, rather than mediocrity, and dynamism, rather than

lethargy, are the main thrusts that need to be subtly interwoven into the fabric of Islamic education.

(Omer, 2019)

Integration, etymologically, it comes from the Latin word *integer* or *integrare*, which means "made whole" (www.etymonline.com). In the context of this book, knowledge integration is referred as the combination of revealed and existential knowledge to form a synthesis of knowledge. That is the consideration of the two sources of knowledge that form the holistic nature of knowledge. In the context of education, this unity of knowledge "is part of what could be called institutional ideological harmony which translates itself into comprehensive integration of curricula, policies, philosophies, values, worldviews and teaching methods" (Omer, 2019). This integration of knowledge, especially the revealed and the created knowledge, is a necessity that will bring balance to the understanding of reality and truth.

That integral unity and hierarchal nature of knowledge, from an Islāmic perspective, are based on revelation, inspiration, intuition, perception and rationality. Knowledge gained from sense perception and rationalism (logical reasoning) should not be neglected. Giving priority to revelation does not debase science, knowledge, empiricism, intuition and reason. However, scientific evidence would be judged and evaluated according to the criteria of divine revelation. This means that revealed knowledge must act both as a guardian and foundation for scientific knowledge. In Islāmic thought, there is no dichotomy, and absolutely no contradiction, between transmitted, divine knowledge from the Qur'ān and Hādīth and the rational, empirical knowledge as both approaches are from the same source, that is, God the Almighty. Enquiring or probing is permissible in Islām so as to arrive at the truth (Leaman, 2006, p. 571). The study of both Qur'ān/Hādīth and scientific knowledge should not be detached or separated, but rather the knowledge of these disciplines should be integrated. From a historical perspective, the notion of knowledge integration seems to be supported and implemented by early classical Muslim scholars in their quest for knowledge during the Islāmic renaissance and beyond. Malkawi (2014) suggested that the classical Muslim scholars, despite their different schools of thought, agreed that

> knowledge should be interconnected, complementary, and organically linked to the knowledge of God. In the view of these scholars, the fact that all sciences originate from a single divine source is the foundation for the ultimate integration and unity of knowledge.
>
> (p. 12)

It has been noted that classical Islāmic scholars "combine three aspects in scientific integration efforts, namely; spiritual, intellectual, and moral. [For example], Ibn Khaldun explained that human science is a natural human

8 *Shifting the paradigm*

phenomenon which originates from two main references, revelation and the universe" (Pulungan & Kalsum, 2019, p. 45).

In fact, the Islāmic principle of divine oneness, or *Tawhîd*, the unity of the source of knowledge and epistemological integration (Malkawi, 2014), constitutes a frame of reference and foundation for a monotheistic Islāmic psychology.

Islāmic monotheism as the foundation of Islāmic psychology

The concept of monotheism (known as *Tawhîd* in Arabic) is the single most important concept in Islām and is the foundation of Islāmic psychology. Three themes that preponderate in Islāmic monotheism are the oneness of God in His lordship (known as *Tawhîd ar-Ruboobeeyah*), the devotion of all worship to God alone (known as *Tawhîd al-'Ibādah*), and the oneness of God in His names and attributes (known as *Tawhîd al-Asmaa was-Sifaat*). However, no psychology can claim to be Islāmic if any of the foundations of the articles of faith are ignored (Lakhin, 2022). The articles of faith include the belief in one God (*Tawhîd*), belief in His angels (*Malaikah*), belief in His books (*Kutub*), belief in the prophets (*Nubuwwah*), belief in the last day and the afterlife (*Akhirah*), and belief in predestination (*Al Qadr*) (see Rassool, 2023). Daud (1989) states,

> The most important aspect of God in the Qur'ān is His Oneness, the affirmation of which became the most fundamental aspect of Islāmic teachings, that is, *Tawhîd*. The spiritual, intellectual, and socio-moral implications of this concept can be obtained both from the Qur'ān itself as well as through logical deduction.
>
> (p. 11)

Islāmic psychology is established on an Islāmic worldview (*Tasawur or Ru'yah al-Islām li al-Wujud*) which is based on the Qur'ān and Sunnah and the Qur'ānic civilization (Nursi, 2011, pp. 745–746). In addition to its Tawhîdic dimension, there is also an ethical (moral, *akhlāq*) dimension of Islāmic worldview which forms the fundamental principles of the paradigm of Islāmic psychology. These principles permeate all topics that pertain to the knowledge and methodology of Islāmic psychology (see Table 1.1).

The principles presented in Table 1.1 define the paradigm of Islāmic psychology, which has a completely different approach and methodology in contrast with Judeo-Christian or secular psychology in the study of human behaviours and experiences. Rassool (2023) maintains,

> The methodology of study it is not limited to the sphere of knowledge gained from sense perception and rationalism (logical reasoning). It is also

deal with the supernatural phenomena of the invisible world which cannot be measured or evaluated using the means of empiricism, intuition, and reason. This knowledge it is more extensive than the visible world and is based from divine revelation.

(p. x)

Thus, Islāmic psychology is underpinned by an Islāmic epistemological, ontological and metaphysical worldview and based on the religion of monotheism, according to the creed of *Ahlus-Sunnah Wal-Jamā'ah*. In the context of this book, Islāmic psychology is defined as "the study of the science of the soul, mental processes, and behaviour according to the principles of empirical psychology, rationality and divine revelation from the Qur'ān and Sunnah" (Rassool, 2023, p. x).

Table 1.1 Paradigm of Islāmic psychology

Beliefs framework	Explanation
Belief in monotheism	*Tawhîd*
Belief in Allāh as the as the only Creator and Sustainer of everything	The only One who is worthy of worship
Belief in the six axioms of the articles of faith	*Imān*, known as *Arkān al-īmān*
Belief that man is part of the universe created by Allāh	Part of the cosmos ruled by Allāh
Belief in the covenant with Allāh	See Qur'ān 7:172.
Belief in the religious characteristics	Connection with belief in the supernatural and invisible world
Belief in the metaphysical component of the self: *Qalb* (heart), *Rūḥ* (soul), *Nafs* (desire-nature) and *Aql* (intellect, reason)	Each of these terms signifies a spiritual entity.
Belief in the fundamentals of Islāmic anthropology	The concept of *Fitrah*
Adopting the Prophet Muhammad ﷺ as a role model	Having an outstanding character (*khuluqyl 'adhiym*) and following his Sunnah
Belief in divine revelation as a source of knowledge	Knowledge of hidden world and about the nature, meaning and purpose of life
Belief in knowledge integration	Integrated knowledge and integrated research as a methodology in Islāmic psychology
Belief in the holistic dimension of Islāmic psychology	Biological, social, psychological and spiritual dimensions
Belief in psychosocial and spiritual interventions	Congruent with Islāmic beliefs and practices

Source: Adapted from Rassool (2023)

Problems and limitations of secular psychology

Secularism has been embedded in mainstream psychology due to the separation of religion and science. This means that "religious ideas, practice, and organizations lose their influence in the face of scientific and other knowledge" (McLeish, 1995, p. 668). In this context, the focus of academic discourse, theories and approaches and the development of the different schools of thought were rooted in 19th century, with the rationalist philosophical paradigm being incompatible to religion and spirituality (Rose, 1998). Thus, the practice of religiosity often subjugates the autonomy of thought and action and results in closed-mindedness and developmental stagnation. Religious thought and ideas ought to be rejected and treated by academics as oppressive and/or irrelevant holdovers from an earlier, more primitive stage of society (de la Chaumiere, 2004).

From a historical perspective, the study of the soul held prominent place in discussions related to psychology before the separation of science and religion and the emergence of Western scientific paradigm. Psychology, etymologically, means the science of the soul; that is, *psyche* means "breath, spirit, soul" and *logia* means "study of" or "research" (Etymonline, 2020). The emphasis on the secularisation of modern psychology is based on the premise that religion is based on faith, which cannot be evaluated by objective methods, whereas science is based on empiricism and experimentation in order to establish facts that are verifiable. It has been suggested that "although secularisation has changed the nature and quality of the relationship between psychology and religion it has not undone the relationship altogether. Religion still matters for many people, including psychologists, at some level" (Reber, 2006, p. 194). However, despite the uneasy co-existence between psychology and religion, spirituality and religion still matter and are embedded in the worldview of many people. It has been suggested that the discipline of psychology has been subjected with several interwoven crises for decades. Hughes has highlighted that the crises in secular psychology include theoretical fragmentation (a paradigmatic crisis), reductionism (a measurement crisis), sloppy approaches to significance and effect sizes (a statistical crisis), a tendency to focus on a limited sample of the human population (a sampling crisis) and the premature optimism about the progress made by psychology (an identity crisis?).

One of the major crises with secular psychology stems from its failure to recognise peoples' religious experiences and ethical resources. Secular psychology denies the reality of the unconscious and a significant majority deny the reality of the soul. Zarabozo (2002) highlighted the main weaknesses of the secular approaches to psychology:

> Humans are viewed as independent of their Creator and Lord. Theories are based upon human intellect alone, while discounting revelation from the Creator. Knowledge and research focus only on the tangible aspects of

humans, while ignoring the spiritual and unseen elements. Behaviours are generally seen to be determined solely by drives, reflexes, conditioning, and social influences.

(p. 49)

Secular contemporary psychology has been promoted on a global scale, and its dominance has remained unchallenged in most academic institutions in the developing world, especially in Muslim-majority countries. For many Muslim psychologists, relying on Islāmic theology is tantamount to being unscientific: "They prided themselves as scientists being guided by a neutral value-free scientific method in which there was no room for religious 'dogma'" (Badri, cited in Khan, 2015, p. 161). The problem with secular psychologists is the position Muslim psychologist in the 'lizard hole' by their failure to include ethical behaviours or ethical intelligence within the paradigm of secular psychology. The following Hādīth illustrates this point. It was narrated from Abu Hurairah that the Messenger of Allāh ﷺ said: "You will most certainly follow the ways of those who came before you, arm's length by arm's length, forearm's length by forearm's length, hand span by hand span, until even if they entered a hole of a *mastigure* (lizard) you will enter it too." They said: "O Messenger of Allah, (do you mean) the Jews and the Christians?" He said: "Who else?" (Ibn Majah).

Another point of contention with secular psychology is that despite their recognition of the inclusion of code of ethics for therapy or research involving animals or human participants, they still reject human ethics and values to form part of the dimensions of psychology. A more integrated psychology of the 21st century, rather than being stuck in their colonial and Orientalist past, would have ethics and human values of what is right or wrong or what is good or evil "as philosophical and religious issues like ethics, human values, aesthetics, and the nature of life have everything to do with psychology" (Reber, 2006, p. 200). The main limitation of contemporary secular psychology is presented in Table 1.2.

Table 1.2 Limitations of secular psychology

Authors	Limitations of secular psychology
Badri (1979)	Failure to include the spiritual side of man
D'Souza and Rodrigo (2004)	Lack of cultural sensitivity and competence in dealing with clients' religious beliefs and practices
James (1902/1999)	Excluding religious experience will be an incomplete psychology.
Rassool (2021)	Psychology is devoid of the soul as part of human nature.
Reber (2006)	Incomplete psychology (p. 196) Exclusion of ethics, human values (p. 200)

(*Continued*)

12 Shifting the paradigm

Table 1.2 (Continued)

Authors	Limitations of secular psychology
Richards and Bergin (2005)	Scientific naturalism does not adequately account for the complexities and mysteries of life and of the universe (p. 37).
Zarabozo (2002)	Humans are viewed as independent of their Creator and Lord.
	Theories are based on human intellect alone while discounting revelation from the Creator.
	Knowledge and research focus only on the tangible aspects of humans while ignoring the spiritual and unseen elements.
	Behaviours are generally seen to be determined solely by drives, reflexes, conditioning and social influences (p. 49).
	Dangers of fabricated or secular theories: leading people to the wrong path for spiritual purification (pp. 44–45)
Utz (2011)	The secular definition of psychology assumes that we were put in this world and left to our own devices, without any divine intervention (p. 29).

Source: Adapted from Rassool (2021)

However, Reber (2006) recommends, that an integration of religion and psychology would require a combination of the common values, ethics and worldviews of both disciplines that are mutually ideal for studying human behaviours and experiences.

Colonisation and globalisation of psychology

Psychological knowledge has been increasingly criticised for their Orientalist and Eurocentric perspectives and biases due to colonisation and globalisation. Scholars have argued that mainstream psychological knowledge is based on a "psychological imperialism" that undermines the indigenous knowledge and this knowledge has been created by and for Euro-US consumptions (Bhatia, 2017; Owusu-Bempah & Howitt, 2000). The colonisation of psychology, as a hegemonic standard for academic work and clinical practice, is based on the notion rooted in individualistic values that are Western, educated, industrial, rich, and democratic (WEIRD) (Henrich et al., 2010), out of which Western psychology and its clinical branches emerged. It has been argued that

> [s]ince the end of the colonial period, epistemologies and knowledge systems at our universities have not changed considerably; they remain rooted in colonial and Western-centric worldviews. The curriculum remains largely Eurocentric and continues to reinforce white and

Western dominance and privilege, while at the same time being full of stereotypes, prejudices and patronising views about non-white people and cultures.

(Keele University, 2018)

This "White curriculum" (Peters, 2018) is based on "Whiteness as the ideology and way of being in the world that is used to maintain White supremacy" (Picower, 2009, p. 198). The "Whiteness curriculum" contents of psychology programmes, in both universities and academic institutions in the West and countries with large Muslim majorities, hold ramifications for students in relation to the Eurocentric psychological knowledge and clinical practice. In addition, the whiteness of curriculum contents in psychology is being presented as race-neutral and universal (Bhatia, 2017), with *white* practices being framed as the *right* practices (Gillborn, 2021, p. 28) and the legitimate producer of knowledge (Johnson & Joseph-Salisbury, 2018). The evidence of colonial impact can be seen in mapping the growth and expansion of hegemonic psychology in undergraduate and postgraduate courses in post-colonial Muslim countries.

There is the view that globalisation is the new façade of colonisation and is opened to the same criticism. Psychology and applied psychology have become a global enterprise can no longer be dissociated from the global sociocultural and political context that frames the lives of the global communities. This is reflected in the following statements:

Psychological globalisation embraces every country throughout the world and is crystalised as "The Three Worlds of Psychology." In this theory, the United States is considered the first world because to date it is the major producer of psychological knowledge that is exported to both the second world of psychology (e.g., England, Canada, and Australia) and the third world of psychology (i.e., developing countries such as Nigeria, Cuba). This theory presumes that each of the three worlds has an unequal capacity to produce and disseminate psychological knowledge that shapes the field of psychology.

(Lawson et al., 2007, p. 8)

The problematic influences of globalisation in regard to cross-cultural psychological practices have been identified. According to Watters (2010),

America has been the world leader in generating new mental health treatments and modern theories of the human psyche. We export our psycho-pharmaceuticals packaged with the certainty that our biomedical knowledge will relieve the suffering and stigma of mental illness. We categorise disorders, thereby defining mental illness and health, and then parade these seemingly scientific certainties in front of the world.

The global and wholesale importation of psychology knowledge and clinical practice, alien to Islāmic culture, have shaped the Muslim psychologists' perception and worldview of their professional practice. The challenges faced by post-colonial Muslim-majority countries have primed Muslim pedagogics to develop new frameworks to incorporate the traditional forms of Islāmic education with the Western knowledge, in the form of Islāmisation of knowledge. In reality, despite the significant influence of the Islāmisation of knowledge and the Islāmic psychology movements and the development of pseudo-conceptual framework in Islāmic psychology and psychotherapy, there is still a dearth of literature on epistemological and pedagogical discourse in knowledge integration of Islāmic ethics and sciences in the curriculum at undergraduate and postgraduate levels and in continuing professional development courses.

Decolonising psychology knowledge

There has been a propagation of the literature focusing on the decolonisation of psychological science (Adams et al., 2015; Adams et al., 2018; Dudgeon & Walker, 2015; Gómez-Ordóñez et al., 2021; Rassool, 2020, 2022). Despite the paradigm shift for an Islāmic psychology gathering momentum in the 1980s to replace mainstream psychology, the decolonisation of psychology knowledge and the "White curriculum" are still in existence in most universities in Muslim countries. It is argued that more integrated psychology of the 21st century, rather than being stuck in their colonial and Orientalist past, would have ethics and human values of what is right or wrong or what is good or evil "as philosophical and religious issues like ethics, human values, aesthetics, and the nature of life have everything to do with psychology" (Reber, 2006, p. 200). In the context of Islāmic psychology, the decolonisation of psychology knowledge is

> the process of embedding an Islāmic epistemologies, knowledge systems, theories, research and clinical practices in empirical psychology disciplines. In other words, it is about balancing the secular psychology narratives with Islāmic psychology, ethics and sciences while both evidenced-based psychological knowledge and Islāmic intellectual tradition are maintained.
>
> (Rassool, 2021. p. 583)

Decolonisation of psychological knowledge refers to the undoing of Orientalist and Eurocentric worldview of psychology or the "freeing of minds" from colonial ideology and supremacy. It is shifting the paradigm of secular and Western knowledge in psychological sciences to be more attuned to psychological knowledge based on Indigenous religio-cultural worldview.

Adams et al. (2015) have proposed two conceptual frameworks that inform the approach to decolonising psychological science: the theoretical perspectives of liberation psychology (Martín-Baró, 1994) and cultural psychology (Shweder, 1990). In order to dismantle Eurocentric-US psychology knowledge in institutions, some of the approaches of reclaiming psychology include diversification of knowledge, indigenisation of knowledge and knowledge integration. Diversification of psychology knowledge means addressing the impact and importance of race and diversity to understand human behaviours and experiences; otherwise, it can be argued that psychology is incomplete. In the context of psychology, diversification of knowledge broadly means to modify the curriculum content. However, it has been argued that "decolonising the curriculum moves beyond diversification to a deeper interrogation of the knowledges and biases (re)produced in education" (Gillborn et al., p. 5). Despite the move towards multicultural competence becoming a defining feature of psychological practice, education and training, and research (Boysen, 2011; Kite & Littleford, 2013), the findings from a study showed that the psychology curricula are marked by knowledges that (re)produce racism, and there is confusion over whose responsibility for the change lies (Gillborn et al., 2021). The authors concluded that "this analysis has important implications for the perpetuation of institutional racism within psychology, academia in general, and subsequent professional psychological practice" (p. 2).

In the context of Islāmic psychology, diversification of psychology knowledge is the first stage, but it does not resolve the problem of the "soullessness of Western psychology." This position is made clear by Badri (1979), stating,

> There is no mention at all of the other aspects of man. The religious, the spiritual or at least the transcendental. Criteria which fail to include the spiritual side of man can only find anchorage in a society blinded by materialism. In such a society, the behaviour of spiritually motivated practising individuals may brand them as misfits, eccentrics or abnormal.
>
> (p. 24)

Indigenisation of knowledge is another approach in the process of decolonisation of hegemony psychology. This is a process of enabling the psychological disciplines to reflect local context of culture and wisdom. Sinha (1993) discussed two routes indigenisation of psychology: endogenous (culture-oriented and based on religio-philosophical traditions) and exogenous (indigenous culture amalgamated external cultural variables). The exogenous approach operates with the framework of Western psychology but with some adaptations of the theories, methods and approaches. There are inherent problems associated with attempts to indigenise psychology "from within" or "from without" (endogenous and exogenous, respectively). Long (2014) argues that "indigenisation from without" is a paradox because "Western psychology is saturated in a secular metatheory that cannot accommodate the

Islāmic worldview; any attempted revision must remain, in spirit, no different from the original articulation" (p. 17). He also articulates that the "indigenisation from within" approach from those Muslims, without professional training in psychology, solely focuses "on the details of Islāmic spirituality to the virtual exclusion of the secular discipline. In these cases, it is not psychology that is being Islāmised but Islāmic spirituality that is being advocated" (p. 17). Thus, attempts to indigenise psychology knowledge "from within" or "from without" is fraught with obstacles, as Rassool (2021) posited that it is like being in between "Scylla and Charybdis."[1]

The more operational and practical approach is knowledge integration – that is, integrating Islāmic sciences, ethics and worldview with classical and contemporary knowledge of psychology. Both evidenced-based psychological knowledge and Islāmic traditions based on the Qur'ān and Sunnah are maintained in the curriculum contents. Even though Islāmic theology and psychology differ from their sources of knowledge and methodologies, they both share common concerns and elements of focus, such as humanity, purpose, meaning, perspectives on spirituality, suffering, morality and

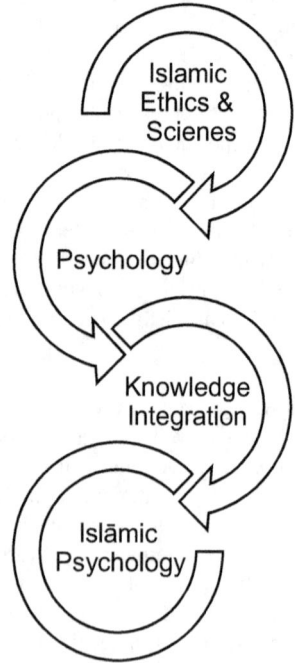

Figure 1.3 A simple model of Islāmic psychology

human potential. However, the Qurʾān and Sunnah offer a reflection of psychology so that it can have a better understanding human behaviours and experiences. Despite the "Islāmisation of knowledge" movement and the evolution and development of Islāmic psychology as a discipline, there has been limited integration of knowledge of Islāmic traditions and perspectives in the psychology curriculum in the different educational institutions around the globe. Haque (2018) maintains, "Whatever integration you will see is largely a copy of the concept and practices of integration in the West." For Islāmic psychology to emerge as a force majeure, there is a need to challenge educationalists with the task of decolonising curriculum contents and integrate Islāmic traditions in psychology programmes. The objective of knowledge integration is to advance a new paradigm that views psychology and the spiritual dimension of human nature not as two opposing fields but as complementary and holistic approaches in the understanding human behaviours and experiences. Figure 1.3 presents a simple model of decolonising psychology.

Challenges to knowledge integration strategy

However, knowledge integration faces a number of obstacles and challenges. In the current climate, there are significant oppositions from Muslims psychologists to the Islāmisation of psychology or knowledge integration especially in Muslim-majority countries. Rassool (2021) suggests that the introduction of Islāmic ethics and sciences in the psychology curriculum is anathema to those Muslim academic psychologists

> who perceived, like the orientalists and Eurocentric, that Islāmic psychology is a form of religio-psychology or "theological scholarship" which is totally at odds with contemporary definitions of psychology. Their rejection is based on the premise that psychology as a science is based on a number of key characteristics: empiricism, determinism, falsifiability, a natural science perspective, etc. Thus, the enactment of these activities defines a scientific study of mind and behaviour and they are not part of any religious system of which Islam is one.
>
> (p. 584)

He reiterated that the anti-Islāmic psychology movement claims that "religio-psychology places contemporary psychology in a subservient position to theology and one returns the study of mind and behaviour to the middle ages" (p. 584). The dilemma of Muslim psychologists is also articulated by Skinner (2019), who points out that Muslim psychologists "have also experienced a dissonance between what they have been taught from 'Western' tradition and their own sense of what is right and real-but without being able to articulate precisely where the dissonance lies" (p. 1088). According to Waheed and Skinner (2022),

> this dissonance often plays out in one of two ways: (i) the social context in which Muslims are placed forces them to assimilate with the dominant psychology culture, but with the sacrifice of their own attitudes, beliefs and values; or (ii) Muslims separate themselves in order to hold on to their own beliefs and values.

There is a duality of roles and beliefs between the personal and the professional. Changing attitude and cognitive dissonance are of upmost priority.

Against this background, we are faced with other challenges to overcome. Muslim psychology lecturers are generally trained to teach sub-disciplines of secular psychology, and the integration of Islāmic sciences and psychology do not fit in "naturally" within their teaching framework and methodologies. Despite the religiosity of some of Muslim psychology lecturers in their personal lives, they have not been prepared to modify the curriculum and integrate or teach Islāmic sciences and psychology. There may also be a reluctance on their part because of negative perception towards Islāmic psychology. In fact, some may even explicitly reject such inclusion because of their acculturation of Western values and secular attitudes.

There is also the issue of attitude, knowledge, and skills commitment (Islāmic commitment) of Muslim psychologists. This "Islāmic commitment" incorporates the evaluation of whether Muslim psychologists have adequate knowledge, training and experience to decolonise psychology knowledge. This led to the problems of role legitimacy, role adequacy and role support. Role legitimacy is the belief that whether they have a legitimate right to change and modify psychology knowledge and integrate Islāmic psychology and ethics. In most cases, this particular role is not part of their job descriptions or responsibilities. Role adequacy refers how knowledgeable Muslim psychologists are about Islamic psychology and Islamic sciences. (Rassool, 2021, p. 603). The problems of role legitimacy, role adequacy and role support are examined in Chapter 5.

One of most important tasks is to undertake a review of the academic curriculum in psychology. The main quandary in reviewing the undergraduate or postgraduate psychology curriculum is whose responsibility is it anyway. However, it is assumed that many universities and academic departments of psychology and accrediting bodies in Muslim countries may be reluctant or evade the responsibility to introduce Islāmic psychology while positioning this as within the other's authority and responsibility. This is diffusion of responsibility. The strategy here cannot be a top-down approach or a bottom-up approach but a collaborative approach. This entails that policy, strategy and implementation of knowledge integration of Islāmic ethics and Islāmic psychology in the psychology curriculum should be a collaborative approach. In fact, it is accrediting bodies or the academic council of universities that shape what content courses must be included to offer accreditation or validation. The challenges and solutions are with those institutions.

Conclusion

For Islāmic psychology to emerge as a force majeure in Muslim-majority countries, there is a need to challenge educationalists and clinicians with the task of decolonising curriculum contents in psychology programmes. This is the prime step towards broader decolonisation of clinical assessment and therapeutic interventions. The occupation of mind by European colonisation (Bulham, 1985) has led Muslim psychologists to follow "His Master's Voice" in "propounding theories of personality, motivation and behaviour which are in many ways contradictory to Islam" (Badri, 2016). Badri (2016) goes on to argue,

> These theories and their applications are carefully sugar-coated with the attractive cover of "science" . . . leads many of them [Muslim psychologists] to accept blindly, consciously and unconsciously, and at times dogmatically, theories and practices that are, to say the least, unsuitable for application in their Muslim countries.
>
> (pp. 2–3)

I called this a form of psychological *Taqleed* – that is, the blind following of secular psychology by Muslim psychologists. For knowledge integration and the teaching of Islāmic psychology and Islāmic ethical values in the psychology curriculum in educational institutions to be successful, factors determining the readiness to integrate, both on individual and institutional levels, need to be established and managed effectively before the implementation process commences. The ultimate goal is to prepare clinicians with the best approaches to deal with psychosocial and spiritual problems faced by the Muslim *Ummah* (community).

Note

1 An idiom derived from Greek mythology, which means choosing the lesser of two evils.

Bibliography

Adams, G., Dobles, I., Gómez, L., Kurtiş, T., & Molina, L.E. (2015). Decolonizing Psychological Science: Introduction to the Special Thematic Session. *Journal of Social and Political Psychology*, 3(1), 213–238.

Adams, G., Estrada-Villalta, S., & Gómez Ordóñez, L.H. (2018). The Modernity/Coloniality of Being: Hegemonic Psychology as Intercultural Relations. *International Journal of Intercultural Relations*, 62, 13–22.

Badri, M.B. (1979). *The Dilemma of Muslim Psychologists*. London: MWH.

Badri, M.B. (2016). *The Dilemma of Muslim Psychologists*. Kula Lumpur: Islāmic Book Trust.

Bhatia, S. (2017). *Decolonizing Psychology: Globalization, Social Justice, and Indian Youth Identities*. Oxford: Oxford University Press.

Boysen, G.A. (2011). Diversity Topics Covered in Teaching of Psychology Courses. *Teaching of Psychology*, 38(2), 89–93.

Bulhan, H.A. (1985). *Frantz Fanon and the Psychology of Oppression*. New York: Plenum Press.

Daud, W.M.N. (1989). *The Concept of Knowledge in Islam: And Its Implication for Education in a Developing Country*. New York: Mansell Publishing Limited.

de la Chaumiere, R. (2004). *What's It All About? A Guide to Life's Basic Questions and Answers*. Wisdom House Press.

D'Souza, R. F., & Rodrigo, A. (2004). Spiritually augmented cognitive behavioural therapy. *Australasian psychiatry: bulletin of Royal Australian and New Zealand College of Psychiatrists*, 12(2), 148–152. https://doi.org/10.1080/j.1039-8562.2004.02095.x.

Dudgeon, P., & Walker, R. (2015). Decolonising Australian Psychology: Discourse, Strategies, and Practice. *Journal of Social and Political Psychology*, 3(1), 276–297. http://doi.org/10.5964/jspp.v3i1.126.

Etymonline (2020). Retrieved on 15 Nay 2023 from https://www.etymonline.com/search?q=psychology.

Gillborn, S., Woolnough, H., Jankowski, G., & Sandle, R. (2021). "Intensely White": Psychology Curricula and the (Re)Production of Racism. *Educational Review*. https://doi.org/10.1080/00131911.2021.1978402 (accessed 12 September 2022).

Gómez-Ordóñez L., Adams, G., Ratele, K., Suffla, S., Stevens, G., & Reddy, G. (2021). Decolonising Psychological Science: Encounters and Cartographies of Resistance. *The Psychologist*, September, 54–57.

Haque, A. (2018). *Integration of Psychology and Theology*. Paper Presented at the Faculty of Theology, Aligarh Muslim University on the 1st of January 2018.

Henrich, J., Heine, S.J., & Norenzayan, A. (2010). The Weirdest People in the World? *Behavioral and Brain Sciences*, 33(2–3), 61–83.

Hughes, B. (2018). *Psychology in Crisis*. London: Palgrave.

Ibn Kathir. (2000). *Tafsir Ibn Kathir*. Translated by J. Abualrub, N. Khitab, H. Khitab, A. Walker, M. Al-Jibali, & S. Ayoub. Saudi Arabia: Darussalam Publishers and Distributors.

Ibn Majah. *Sunan Ibn Majah 225*. In-book reference: Introduction, Ḥadīth 225 English translation: Vol. 1, Book 1, Ḥadīth 225. Sahih (Darussalam).

Ibn Majah. *Sunan Ibn Majah 3994*. In-book reference: Book 36, Ḥadīth 69.English translation: Vol. 5, Book 36, Ḥadīth 3994. Hasan (Darussalam).

James, W. (1902/1999). *The Varieties of Religious Experience*. New York: Modern Library.

Johnson, A., & Joseph-Salisbury, R. (2018). "Are You Supposed to Be in Here?" Racial Microaggressions and Knowledge Production in Higher Education. In J. Arday & H.S. Mirza (Eds.), *Dismantling Race in Higher Education*. Basingstoke: Palgrave Macmillan, pp. 143–160.

Keele University. (2018).*Decolonising the curriculum network. Keele's Manifesto for Decolonising the Curriculum*. Keele's Student Union , Keele Postgraduate Association and Keele's University College Union. www.keele.ac.uk/equalitydiversity/equalityframeworksandactivities/equalityawardsandreports/equalityawards/raceequalitycharter/keeledecolonisingthecurriculumnetworknline (accessed 13 September 2022).

Khan, R.K. (2015). An Interview with Professor Malik Badri about His Contributions to the Islamisation of Psychology. *Intellectual Discourse*, 23(1), 159–172.

Kite, M.E., & Littleford, L.N. (2013). Teaching About Diversity Across the Undergraduate Psychology Curriculum. In D.S. Dunn (Ed.), *The Oxford Handbook of Undergraduate Psychology Education*. Oxford Library of Psychology (online ed.). Oxford Academic. https://doi.org/10.1093/oxfordhb/9780199933815.013.012 (accessed 13 September 2022).

Lakhin, F. (2022). *Islāmic Psychology: Islāmic Monotheism as the Foundation of Islāmic Psychology*. Cited from course in Islāmic psychology. IKI Academy. ITKI 6206 (accessed 8 September 2022).

Lawson, R.B., Graham, J.E., & Baker, K.M. (2007). Contemporary Psychology: Global Forces. In R.B. Lawson, J.E. Graham, & K.M. Baker (Eds.), *A History of Psychology: Globalization, Ideas, and Applications* (1st ed.). New York: Routledge.

Leaman, O. (Ed.). (2006). *The Qur'ān: An Encyclopedia*. Oxford: Routledge.

Long, W. (2014). Critical Reflections on the Islāmicisation of Psychology. *Revelation and Science*, 4, 14–19.

Malkawi, F.H. (2014). *Epistemological Integration: Essentials of an Islāmic Methodology*. Herndon, VA: The International Institute of Islāmic Thought.

Martín-Baró, I. (1994). *Writings for a Liberation Psychology*. Edited by A. Aron & S. Corne. Cambridge, MA: Harvard University Press.

McLeish, K. (1995). *Key Ideas in Human Thought*. New York: Prima Publishing.

Nursi, B.Z. (2011). *The Flashes. [3rd Volume of the Risale-i Nur Collection* (5th ed.). Istanbul, Turkey: Sozler Publications.

Omer, S. (2019). *Integration of Knowledge as a Way Forward*. IslamiCity. www.islamicity.org/19847/integration-of-knowledge-as-a-way-forward/ (accessed 24 October 2022).

Owusu-Bempah, K., & Howitt, D. (2000). *Psychology Beyond Western Perspectives*. Oxford: Wiley.

Peters, M.A. (2018). Why Is My Curriculum White? A Brief Genealogy of Resistance. In J. Arday & H. Mirza (Eds.), *Dismantling Race in Higher Education*. Champ: Palgrave Macmillan. https://doi.org/10.1007/978-3-319-60261-5_14.

Picower, B. (2009). The Unexamined Whiteness of Teaching: How White Teachers Maintain and Enact Dominant Racial Ideologies. *Race Ethnicity and Education*, 12(2), 197–215.

Pulungan, J.S., & Kalsum, N.U. (2019). The Philosophical Transformation of Scientific Paradigm (Study of the Integration of Knowledge in the Perspective of the Qur'ān). *American Journal of Humanities and Social Sciences Research*, 3(12), 49–59.

Ragab, A. (1999). On the Methodology of Islamizing the Social Sciences. *Intellectual Discourse*, 7(1), 27–52.

Rahmattullah Khan Abdul Wahab Khan. (2005). An interview with Professor Malik Badri about his contributions to the Islamisation of psychology. *Intellectual Discourse*, 23(1), 159–172.

Rassool, G.H. (2020). Cognitive Restructuring of Psychology: The Case for a Vertical and Horizontal Integrated, Embedded Curriculum Model for Islāmic Psychology. *Islāmic Studies*, 59(4), 477–494.

Rassool, G.H. (2021). Decolonising Psychology and its (Dis) Contents. In G.H. Rassool (Eds.), *Islāmic Psychology: Human Behaviour and Experiences from an Islāmic Perspective*. Oxford: Routledge, pp. 583–601.

Rassool, G.H. (2022). *Foundation of Islāmic Psychology: From Classical Scholars to Contemporary Thinkers*. Oxford: Routledge.

Rassool, G.H. (2023). *Islāmic Psychology: The Basics*. Oxford: Routledge.

Reber, J.S. (2006). Secular Psychology: What's the Problem? *Journal of Psychology and Theology*, 34(3), 193–204. https://doi.org/10.1177/009164710603400302.

Richards, P. S., & Bergin, A. E. (2005). *A Spiritual Strategy for Counseling and Psychotherapy* (2nd ed.). Washington DC: American Psychological Association. http://dx.doi.org/10.1037/11214-000.

Rose, N. (1998). *Inventing Ourselves: Psychology, Power and Personhood*. Cambridge: Cambridge University Press.

Rosenthal, F. (2007). *Knowledge Triumphant. The Concept of Knowledge in Medieval Islam*. Leiden: Brill.

Shweder, R. (2012). Cultural Psychology – What is It? In J. Stigler, R. Schweder, & G. Herdt (Eds.), *Cultural Psychology: Essays on Comparative Human Development*. Cambridge: Cambridge University Press, pp. 1–44.

Sinha, D. (1993). Indigenisation of Psychology in India and Its Relevance. In U. Kim & J.W. Berry (Eds.), *Indigenous Psychologies*. London: Sage, pp. 30–43.

Skinner, R. (2019). Traditions, Paradigms and Basic Concepts in Islāmic Psychology. *Journal of Religion and Health*, 58, 1087–1094.

Sue, D.W., Bingham, R.P., Porché-Burke, L., & Vasquez, M. (1999). The Diversification of Psychology: A Multicultural Revolution. *The American Psychologist*, 54(12), 1061–1069.

Tirmidhi. *Jami' at-Tirmidhi 2685*. In-book reference: Book 41, Hādīth 41. English translation: Vol. 5, Book 39, Hādīth 268. Hasan (Darussalam).

Utz, A. (2011). *Psychology from an Islāmic Perspective*. Riyadh: International Islāmic Publishing House.

Waheed, H., & Skinner, R. (2022). Decolonising Psychology: Back to the Future. *The Psychologist*, September 2022, 84–86. www.bps.org.uk/psychologist/decolonising-psychology-back-future (accessed 7 September 2022).

Watters, E. (2010). *Crazy Like Us: The Globalization of the American Psyche*. New York: Simon & Schuster Om.

Williams, M.T. (2020). *Managing Microaggressions: Addressing Everyday Racism in Therapeutic Spaces*. Oxford: Oxford University Press.

WiseInstitute. (2018).*The Essential Sources in Islam*. www.wiserinstitute.com/the-essential-sources-in-islam/ (accessed 9 September 2022).

www.etymonline.com. (n.d.). *Integration*. www.etymonline.com/word/integration (accessed 24 October 2022).

Zarabozo, J. (2002). *Purification of the Soul: Process, Concept, and Means*. Denver, CO: Al-Basheer Company for Publications and Translations.

2 Principles of Islāmic psychology education

Introduction

Education is known as a *teleological* concept, which implies it has an aim or purpose (*telos*). Education is very much influenced by a system of values and the perception of what education *is* but also, and more importantly, what education ought to achieve. The educational system seems to have three concurrent, overlapping aims and perform a number of different functions. The aims of education according to Biesta (2010) is concerned with qualification (acquisition of knowledge and development of skills for a certification), socialisation (development of attitudes, values, and traditions) and subjectification (impact of education on the self and person) Subjectification is "neither a skill or a competence; rather, it is a quality of a person" (Murris & Verbeek, 2014, p. 3). However, Western education system is largely dominated by secularism, *laïcité* (idiosyncratic principle of secularism), Eurocentrism and liberal democracy, which shape the individual ethical and moral values. Besides these,

> the philosophical foundation upon which the Western system of education is built is grossly inimical to the teaching of Islām. Among its inhibitive features that make it incompatible with the teaching of Islām are, the relegation of God to the lowest ebb in its curriculum, excessive materialism, over dependence on contradictory philosophies, a culture of scepticism, absolute dependence on techniques, and tight compartmentalization of disciplines among others.
>
> (Gulzar, 2021)

What is at stake is that the existing conditions in present-day educational institutions in most Muslim countries is still positioned on colonised educational, curriculum which does not truly reflect the indigenous religious beliefs and practices. This means that secular, colonised psychology and other social sciences are disconnected with spirituality and religion.

24 Principles of Islāmic psychology education

The Islāmic educational system is universal and cross all the boundaries of ethnic, racial, national or communal interest. The foundation of this system is based the unicity of God (*Tawhîd*) and focuses on the Qur'ān and Hādīth as the primary sources of knowledge. The process of education is to enhance an Islāmic personality and moral development, enabling Muslims to become becoming good citizens and to contribute to welfare of society and the Muslim communities (*Ummah*). The First World Conference on Muslim Education was organised by King Abdullah Abdulaziz University, Saudi Arabia, in 1977 (12–20 Rabi' al-Thani 1397) and was held in Makkah, with the theme "Basis for an Islāmic Education System." The focus was on addressing globally the multifarious problems facing the education of the Ummah. King Abdul-Aziz University published the proceedings of the conference in six volumes in 1979. The First World Conference on Muslim Education, in 1977, set the aim of Islāmic education:

> Education should aim at the balanced growth of the total personality of Man through the training of Man's spirit, intellect, the rational self, feelings and bodily senses. Education should therefore cater for the growth of Man in all its aspects: spiritual, intellectual, imaginative, physical, scientific, linguistic both individually and collectively and motivate all these aspects towards goodness and the attainment of perfection. The ultimate aim of Muslim education lies in the realisation of complete submission to Allah on the level of the individual, the community and humanity at large.
>
> (Ashraf, 1985, p. 4)

The focus of this chapter is to examine the concept of education in Islām, the philosophical foundation of Islāmic education, the aims and purpose of education and the development of the principles of Islāmic psychology education.

Concepts in Islāmic education

The Second World Conference on Muslim Education, in 1980, jointly organised by Quaid-i-Azam University, Islāmabad, Pakistan, and King Abdul-Aziz University, Saudi Arabia, classified knowledge into perennial and acquired sciences. Perennial knowledge includes the Qur'ān, *Hādīth*, classical Arabic, *Sirah* (life of the Prophet Muhammad), *Usul ul-Fiqh* (Islāmic jurisprudence), Islāmic culture and civilisation, comparative religion and Islāmic metaphysics. Acquired knowledge includes the natural, applied and practical sciences, as well as humanities and the social sciences. True Islāmic education should return to the approach of the integration of knowledge (acquired and perennial) in contrast to the secular, compartmentalised system of education. The comprehensive and integrated concept of Islāmic education encompasses not only the transmission of knowledge (*Ta'lim*), ethical and spiritual nurturing (*Tarbiyah*) and moral discipline (*Ta'dib*). *Ta'lim* is the transmission and

Principles of Islāmic psychology education 25

acquisition of knowledge. There is a famous quote from Imam Al-Ghazâlî regarding the issue of education:

> Be assured that knowledge alone does not strengthen the hand.... Though a man read a hundred thousand scientific questions and understood them or learned them but did not work with them ... They do not benefit him except by working......Knowledge is the tree, and working is its fruit; and though you studied a hundred years and assembled a thousand books, you would not be prepared for the mercy of Allah the Exalted except by working.

The pursuit of knowledge in Islām is not for its own sake but for the benefit of oneself and in the helping others in acknowledging God. According to Halstead (2004), the purpose of seeking knowledge should initiate in the learner a spiritual and moral consciousness, which leads to an increase in faith (*Imaan*), which manifests itself as virtuous actions (*'Amal salih*), leading to certainty (*Yaqeen*), which are all constantly emphasised in the Qur'ān. This is reflected in various verses of the Qur'ān about the possession of faith coupled with virtuous or righteous actions (see Al-Ma'idah 5:93; Al-Kahf 18:107; An-Nur 24:55; and Asr 103:3). It has been suggested that

> *Tarbiyah* could be understood as the type of education that addresses the heart, body, mind and soul of an individual. *Tarbiyah* places God at the centre of the individual's learning experience. The main aim of *tarbiyah* could be summed up as providing Muslims with positive guidance in accordance with the Islāmic traditions that will result in them developing into "good adults" who lead fruitful lives in this world and the hereafter.
>
> (Siddique, 2012)

The process of *Tarbiyah* is to produce the perfect human being (*Insan Kamil*) according to Islāmic tenets. *Ta'dib* is referred to as being disciplined, cultured and well-mannered and is related to the process of character development and good social behaviour. The term *Adab*, meaning "good character and behaviour" and "good manners," is close to the concept of character education. Al-Attas (1984) provides a comprehensive explanation of *Adab* as *Ta'dib*.

> *Adab* as *ta'dib* is a discipline of body, soul and spirit as well, namely a discipline that confirms the recognition and recognition of the right place in relation to physical abilities and potential, intellectuals and spirituality, recognition and recognition of the fact that knowledge and form are arranged hierarchically according to various levels (*Marātib*) and degrees. In *adab* will be reflected justice and wisdom (wisdom). *Adab* includes material and spiritual life. *Adab* also contains invitations to banquets that bring spiritual pleasure, *adab* involves discipline of mind and soul,

right actions and aspects of honour. *Adab*'s emphasis includes charity and knowledge so as to combine science, charity, and manners harmoniously, from these three harmonisations giving birth to *ta'dib* as the terminology of Islāmic education.

(pp. 52–60)

Nata (2013) proposes that the revitalisation of character education be carried out through four points: (1) applying social, emotional, cognitive, physical, moral and spiritual theories in the character educational development; (2) the teaching of morals, values, religious education and civil society; (3) revitalising the role of family, school and society; and (4) revitalising mass media. Halstead (2004) suggests that the three terms *Tarbiyah, Ta'dib* and *Ta'lim* are involved in the Islāmic education process in relation to "(i) aiding individual development, (ii) increasing understanding of society and its social and moral rules and (iii) transmitting knowledge" (p. 522). Thus, these three dimensions form the purpose of Islāmic education.

Philosophy of Islāmic education

An understanding of the philosophy of Islāmic education entails the examination of knowledge drawn from divine revelation, metaphysics, philosophy and axiology, which form the bases of learning, pedagogy and ethics. The philosophy of Islāmic education is

> looking at the principles and concepts underlying education in Islām, it is analysing and criticising, deconstructing and disintegrating of the existing educational infrastructure and strives to produce new concepts continuously or displays what should be the concepts. In this sense it is philosophy that beyond what is existing constantly toward absolute values and is working in the space of Islāmic knowledge and who is humane and moral essence.
>
> (Rayan, 2012, p. 150)

There are several scholars, both classical scholars, including Al-Ghazâlî and Al-Fārābī, and contemporary thinkers, including Al-Attas and Al-Farūqī, who have contributed to philosophy of Islāmic education.

Al-Ghazâlî's philosophy of education is still applicable and relevant in contemporary society. The basic premise of his educational philosophy is the concept of God and His connection with humankind. The aim of education for Al-Ghazâlî is the provision of knowledge of acts of worship (Al-Ghazâlî, 1962) so that man can adhere to the teaching of Islām to obtain salvation and happiness in the hereafter. This means that it is through the process of education and the teachings of religion that assured humankind salvation and happiness in the hereafter. He views education as the development of skills and

Principles of Islāmic psychology education 27

techniques and their relationship between students and teachers "which proceed gradually, developmentally and continuously throughout the student's life, the purpose of which is to cultivate harmoniously" (Alavi, 2007, p. 312). In summary, Al-Ghazâlî's aims in education (Al-Ghazâlî, 1962, 1963; Abu-Sway, 1996) include the following:

- Teachings of religion from happiness and salivation
- Formation of character
- Cleansing the heart, as a result of which the "light of knowledge" will brighten one's heart
- Moral development
- Earning a living
- Societal development and obligation (*Fard-e Kifaya*)

Al-Ghazâlî maintains that education is not merely a process for the impartation of knowledge from the teacher to the student, but rather it is an interaction affecting and benefiting both teacher and student. That is, the teacher gains merit for giving instruction, and the student cultivates himself through the gaining of knowledge. Al-Ghazâlî attaches great importance to the climate in which teaching takes place and the teacher acting as a positive role model. Al-Ghazâlî (1962) also discusses the role of parents in developing a child's initial education in language, cultural traditions, and religious and moral beliefs. The role of teachers is viewed as more critical in the education than the parents, but they both have shared responsibility in the development of character formation. The role of students is also examined, and they should follow the code of ethics, a kind of etiquette in seeking authentic knowledge. Al-Ghazâlî proposes a code of ethics, and this is presented in Table 2.1

Al-Ghazâlî has two dimensions of his curriculum: the obligatory (*Fard-e-Ain*, individual obligation) as the compulsory curriculum, which includes the Qur'ān, logic and hygiene, and the optional (*Fard-e-Kifaya*, community obligation). The role of *adab* (manners, ethics), according to Al-Ghazâlî, is both physical and spiritual education (*ta'dib al-zahir wa al-batin*). It focuses on four facets of a man: his words, deed, faith and motivation (cited in Asmaa Mohd Arshad, 2012, p. 252). The contents of the learning programme include the role of the society and the environment, social psychology and the understanding of child psychology. Al-Ghazâlî emphasises that teaching should be linked to concrete situations, which is having a link between theory and practice and proposes the need for various types of knowledge and skills development. He promotes the idea of the integration of knowledge and the relations between its various filed of knowledge. During the time of Al-Ghazâlî, self-directed learning and lifelong learning were at the vanguard of learning and teaching methodologies, as the educational curriculum was not strictly defined (Abu-Sway, 1996). The methodology of teaching includes

Table 2.1 Al-Ghazâlî's code of ethics for students

	Code of ethics
Ensure	spiritually purity before they undertake the quest for knowledge
Respect	rights of their teachers and behave in a civil manner
Beware	of paying too much attention to doctrinal controversies
Master	the fundamentals of the sciences (linguistics, *Tafsir, Hadith, Fiqh* and *Kalam*), and then specialise by studying one or more of those sciences
Choose	useful subjects in which to specialise, especially those that are conducive to salvation in the hereafter
Study	each subject thoroughly before going on to another, bearing in mind the logical sequence and interconnection of the various disciplines (knowledge integration)
Main goal	Quest for knowledge cultivation and perfection of the innermost self in this world, and closeness to God in the hereafter, rather than the attainment of high office or the acquisition of wealth or fame

Source: Adapted from Al-Ghazâlî (1962)

role modelling, imitation, teacher as role model, relaxation, recreational activities, and encouraging inspiration and reflection but not memorisation (conditioning).

One of the least-known contributors to the philosophy of education is Abū Nasr Al-Fārābī, the classical scholar during the Islāmic renaissance period. Al-Fārābī used a large number of technical terms to describe this concept: discipline (*Ta'dib*), correction/assessment (*Taqwim*), training (*Tahdhib*), guidance (*Tasdid*), instruction (*Ta'lim*), exercise or learning (*Irtiyad*) and upbringing or education (*Tarbiyah*) (Cited in Al-Talbi, 1993, p. 357). In Al-Fārābī's view, the whole activity of education is

> the acquisition of values, knowledge and practical skills by the individual, within a particular period and a particular culture. The goal of education is to lead the individual to perfection since the human being was created for this purpose, and the goal of humanity's existence in this world is to attain happiness, which is the highest perfection-the absolute good.
> (Cited in Al-Talbi, 1993, p. 354)

The perfect human being (*Al insan al kamil*) is the one who has obtained theoretical and practical moral virtue to become perfect in his moral behaviour. In Al-Fārābī's view, one of the goals of education is to combine learning with practical action, which is the strong link between knowledge and action. "Whatever by its nature should be known and practiced, its perfection lies in it actually being practiced" (Al-Fārābī, 1987, p. 73). It has been suggested that Al-Fārābī "is considered to be the first Muslim philosopher to classify the sciences and learning, not just for the sake of enumerating them, but also with an educational objective" (Al-Talbi, 1993, p. 361). Al-Fārābī lays down the conditions of both morality and learning for the teacher and the student. In contrast with other Classical scholars like Al-Ghazâlî, Al-Fārābī does not make learning the Qur'ān and the Islāmic jurisprudence a prerequisite, for he places the learning of religion (*Fiqh*) and theology (*Kalam*) at the end of the curriculum. He also advocates a form of self-directed learning with the proviso of identifying the book's objective, its purpose and its structure, then its relationship to the sciences. He recommends the use of visual aids to complement the oral teaching and the use of imagination. The use of imagination is explained in the use

> geometric shapes drawn upon a board so as to stimulate the imagination, and so that the demonstration itself will not confuse the intellect, and the imagination may be busy with something similar to the thing which it is intended to demonstrate, and will therefore not obstruct the process.
>
> (Al-Fārābī, 1968, p. 94)

Al-Fārābī used a form of operant conditioning in dealing with behavioural problems with positive reinforcement. He values the use of examination in the evaluation of the outcomes of teaching. One of the criticisms about the ideas of Al-Fārābī is the assertion that philosophy is a valid way to understand the meaning of true happiness. This is in contrast with the consensus of scholars who opposed the idea of using philosophy to understand the divine. Religious scholars and theologians have taught that the only way to achieve perfect happiness is to obey the divine law set down in the Qur'ān. Al-Fārābī holds the view that religion is analogous or similar to philosophy and argues that the idea of the true prophet (lawgiver) ought to be the same as that of the true philosopher (king). The theologian Ibn Taymiyyah al-Ḥarrānī (may Allah have mercy upon him), one of the imams of *Ahl al-Sunnah wa'l-Jamaa'ah*, regarded him as being misguided and a disbeliever.

Al-Farūqī's central theme in Islāmic education is the concept of *Tawhîd*. In the context of educational discourse, the concept of *Tawḥīd* "is the affirmation of the unity of the sources of truth. God is the Creator of nature from whence man derives this knowledge" (Al-Farūqī, 1983, p. 45). This worldview of *tawḥīd* "reflects the essence and intrinsic philosophy and paradigm of knowledge rooted on Islāmic vision of reality and truth. It embodies the comprehensive and holistic vision of education that seeks to integrate the fundamental element of revealed and acquired knowledge" (Rahman et al., 2015, p. 235). This is the basis of Islāmic education, which is knowledge that is not fragmented or segmented but integrated – that is, the integration of knowledge that is rational (*'Aqlī*) with the revealed knowledge (*Naqlī*). The fundamental principles and philosophy of education advocated by Al-Farūqī include the following:

- Education is the cornerstone and building block of any state and its crucial foundation and prerequisite. This entails the effort of "educating the mind, reforming the heart and organising the arms (A*l-Arkān)*" (Al-Faruqi, 1981).
- The *Tawḥīdic* principle forms the basic foundation of educational framework that emphasises on the value of truth and knowledge.
- Education is rooted on the classical example of the Muslim-based idea of *Al-Tabyin*, "to make clearly understood" (Rahman et al., 2015, p. 237).
- Free and holistic education must be provided for all, mostly operating at a mosque at any convenient time.
- Divine knowledge and rational knowledge must be integrated.
- There must be a creation of "disciplines that would be at the same time humanistic but would be able to keep into account the communitarian (*Umma*) dimension of the Islāmic model" (Bocca-Aldaqre, 2019, p. 3).

Al-Farūqī's (1982) framework is based on five principles of Islām: oneness of God, unity of creation, unity of truth, unity of life and unity of humanity. Based on these principles, scholars who are responsible for the development of the Islāmisation process need to be experts in modern science and Islāmic knowledge of those fields. There is the relevance of the importance of Islām in modern disciplines and comparing and relating Islāmic values and ethics with modern social sciences. These characteristics were later formulated into a 12-point framework.

Syed Muhammad Naquib Al-Attas, a key figure in "Islāmisation of knowledge" movement has proposed philosophy of Islāmic education based on *Ta'dib* concept, not *Tarbiyah* (Al-Attas, 1999). According to Al-Attas, the concept of *Tarbiyah* is similar with term of Western education (Latin term *educere*) but is not adequate to represent the concept of education in Islām. In contrast, the concept of *Ta'dib* has not only physical and material essence but also have moral and spiritual implications. To this end, Islāmic education is the "recognition and acknowledgement, progressively instilled into man, of the proper places of things in the order of creation, such that it leads to the recognition and acknowledgement of the proper place of God in the order of being and existence" (Al-Attas, 1999, p. 21). Islāmic education focuses on the holistic nature of man and constitutes the spiritual, intellectual, religious, cultural, individual and social dimensions. Thus, the core of Islāmic education must include elements that relate to the nature of the following:

- Religion (*Din*)
- Man (*Insan*)
- Knowledge (*Ilm* and *Ma'rifah*)

- Wisdom (*Hikmah*)
- Justice (*'Adl*)
- Right action (*'Amal* as *Adab*)
- University (*Kulliyyah-Jami'ah*) (Al-Attas, 1979, p. 43)

Al-Attas' (1979) framework of Islāmic education is directed toward the "balanced growth of the total personality . . . through training Man's spirit, intellect, rational self, feelings and bodily senses . . . such that faith is infused into the whole of his personality" (p. 158). The foundation of Islāmic education should be grounded with the concepts of *Tawhîd*, the teaching of the Qur'ān, Shari'ah, and Sunnah. Al-Attas (1979) suggests that the curriculum contents of Islāmic education should include the principles and practice of Islām, the religious sciences (*Uulum al-Shar'iah*), legitimate elements of *Tasawwuf*, psychology, cosmology and ontology, Islāmic philosophy, Islāmic ethics and moral principles and *adab*, knowledge of the Arabic language and the Islāmic worldview (p. 43–44). Ismail (2020) points out, "The underlining of *adab* as Islāmic education by al-Attas is in line with classic Islāmic scholars, especially Al-Ghazâlî" (p. 346).

Rassool (2022) suggests, "In Islāmic educational theory, knowledge is gained in order to actualise the human potential and to perfect (*Ihsan*), the moral character and the holistic dimensions of the nature of man" (p. 223). It seemed that Al-Ghazâlî, Al-Fārābī, Al-Attas and Al-Farūqī shared similar vision in the development of Islāmic education in the integration of Islāmic ethics and sciences, the Qur'ān and Sunnah into education. Nasr (1984) proposes that there is a need for Muslim scholars to integrate positive elements of modern science in which "God reigns supreme" and that the education's "ultimate goal is the abode of permanence and all education points to the permanent world of eternity" (p. 7).

It should be pointed out that philosophers, classical and modern, base their principles into one of the four types or a combination of ontological, anthropological, epistemological and axiological perspectives to guide the principles and practice of an Islāmic philosophy of education. Islāmic philosophy of education aspires to "shape the human being based on matching between the three dimensions of sense, mind and religious faith, In the belief that harmony between those dimensions may achieve the human values in reality" (Rayan, 2012, p. 156). "Education for all" is the motto in Islām. However, the acquisition of knowledge in Islām is not an end in itself but a means for the purification of the soul (*Tazkiyah al-Nafs*).

The purpose of education from an Islāmic perspective

The purpose of Islāmic education is different from secular education. It goes beyond the provision of qualification, socialisation and subjectification (Biesta, 2010), despite its legitimacy in contemporary society. Al-Attas argues,

"The purpose of higher education is not, like in the West, to produce the complete citizen, but rather, as Islām, to produce the complete man, or the universal man" (Ali, 2010, pp. 113–114). The acquisition of knowledge is not the sole purpose of Islāmic education but "to prepare them for a life of purity and sincerity. This total commitment to character-building based on the ideals of Islāmic ethics is the highest goal of Islāmic education (Al-Attas, 1979, p. 104). The purpose of Islāmic education is to make a "balance between three levels: sense, mind and ethics, and promoting them by various educational method" (Rayan, 2012, p. 155). The purpose of education, presented earlier, focused on development of man in all dimensions (spiritual, intellectual, imaginative, physical, scientific, linguistic) with an integrated vision of life to subserve his faith. Applying Cook's (n.d.) notions of education in acquiring intellectual knowledge (through the application of reason and logic) and developing spiritual knowledge (derived from divine revelation and spiritual experience) may be used to form the basis of the of goal of education in Islāmic psychology.

Philosophy of education in Islāmic psychology

There is limited literature on the philosophy of education in Islāmic psychology, with the exception of the works of Rassool (2021, 2022). This philosophy underlies the beliefs, values and understanding of the curriculum approach that is conceptualised in teaching and learning activities. When it comes to curriculum design and development, there is a diversity of views on what is considered to be important and valuable in Islāmic psychology. It is the study of ontology, epistemology and axiology that helps us to understand how the knowledge is constructed and what is considered to be of value. The curriculum in Islāmic psychology is informed by epistemology (knowledge), ontology (nature of reality) and axiology (ethics and values). In the discipline of Islāmic psychology, the ontological dimension what is considered to be real leans towards subjective, objective and divine reality. This dimension also includes the Islāmic worldview. This trinity of realities – subjective, objective and divine – is what determines what truly are the most important aspects to include in the Islāmic psychology curriculum. The axiology dimension on the themes of Islāmic values and ethics, psycho-ethics and moral behaviours heavily influences the way the curriculum contents of the Islāmic psychology is composed. Islāmic ethics can be seen to underpin the entire curriculum. The epistemology dimension is based on the essential knowledge, truth and beliefs. These three dimensions constitute the bases of knowledge integration or the "ethicalisation of psychology" (Ahmad, 2022) in Islāmic psychology curriculum.

An effective educational practice has to be based on a philosophy to guide the curriculum development. Rayan (2012) suggests,

> The philosophy of Islāmic education is looking at the principles and concepts underlying education in Islām; it is analysing and criticising, deconstructing and disintegrating of the existing educational infrastructure and

strives to produce new concepts continuously or displays what should be the concepts. In this sense, it is philosophy that beyond what is existing constantly toward absolute values and is working in the space of Islāmic knowledge and who is humane and moral essence.

(p. 150)

In essence, Islāmic philosophy of education in psychology seeks to understand human nature from a holistic approach based on matching between the three dimensions of mind, body and religious faith (Islām). This relationship is based on the ethical authority of the Qur'ān and Sunnah. Halstead (2004) argues that the social and moral dimension of education in Islām is to understand and adhere to the *Shari'ah*, or divine law, which not only contains universal moral principles but also details instructions relating daily human activities.

Rassool (2021) proposes that the goal of Islāmic education in the study of psychology should be to achieve the following:

- To impart Islāmic ethics and sciences so to enable Muslim psychologists to develop ethical intelligence.
- To be clear in its aims in developing Muslim psychologists professionally and personally in the service of the *Ummah*.
- To impart authentic Islāmic knowledge to Muslim psychologists "that lead human beings towards the consciousness of the Creator in order to obey His commands" (Al-Ghazâlî).
- To provide an increased awareness and recognition of the holistic needs (Bio-psychosocial and spiritual) of Muslim (and non-Muslim) patients or clients.
- To enhance knowledge and evidenced-based intervention strategies required to provide high quality counselling and psychotherapeutic care.
- To develop conceptual framework and curriculum approaches for undergraduate, postgraduate and continuing professional development programmes.
- To develop knowledge and skills in Islāmic thought in the knowledge integration in educational programmes and teaching practices.
- To apply the anthropology and Islām and Islāmic civilisations in the understanding and evolution of Islāmic psychology.
- To develop research skills and cultivating a research-based approach in the provision of evidence to effect change in education and therapeutic interventions.

(p. 587)

A vertical and horizontal integrated, embedded curriculum model of Islāmic psychology was developed and implemented by Rassool (2020) to enable the integration of Islāmic psychology and Islāmic ethical values in psychology knowledge.

Bibliography

Abu-Sway, M.M. (1996). *Al-Ghazzaliy: A Study in Islāmic Epistemology*. Kuala Lumpur: Dewan Bahasa Dan Pustaka.

Ahmad, A. (2022). *Ethicalisation of Social Sciences*. Seminar for the Faculty Capacity Development Programme-IP. Riphah International University, Gulberg Green Campus, Islāmabad, 27 November.

Al-Attas, S.M. al-Naquib (1979). Preliminary Thoughts on the Nature of Knowledge and the Definition and Aims of Education. In *Aims and Objectives of Islāmic Education*. Jeddah and Bucks: King Abdulaziz University and Hodder and Stoughton.

Al-Attas, S.M. al-Naquib. (1984). *Konsep Pendidikan Dalam Islām: Suatu Rangka Pikir Pembinaan Filsafat Pendidikan Islām*. Bandung: Mizan.

Al-Attas, S.M. al-Naquib. (1999). *The Concept of Education in Islām: A Framework for an Islāmic Philosophy of Education*. Kuala Lumpur: ISTAC, p. 12.

Alavi, H.R. (2007). Al-Ghazâlî on Moral Education. *Journal of Moral Education*, 36(3), 309–319.

Al-Fārābī, A.N. (1968). *Al-Alfaz al-musta'mala fil-mantiq*. Edited by Muhsin Mahdi. Beirut: Dar al-Machriq.

Al-Fārābī, A.N. (1987). *Al-Tanbih 'ala sabil al-sa'ada*. Edited by Ja'afar al-Yasin. Beirut: Dar al-Manahil.

Al-Farūqī, I.R. (1981). Islāmizing the Social Science. In I.R. Al-Faruqi & A.O. Nasef (Eds.), *Social and Natural Science*. Jeddah: King Abdul Aziz University.

Al-Farūqī, I.R. (1982). *Islāmization of Knowledge: General Principles and Work Plan*. Herndon, VA: International Institute of Islāmic Thought (IIIT).

Al-Farūqī, I.R. (1983). *Al-Tawhid: Its Implications for Thought and Life*. Kuala Lumpur: International Islāmic Federation of Students Organization.

Al-Ghazâlî, A.H. (1962). *The Book of Knowledge*. Translated by N.A. Faris. New Delhi: Islāmic Book Services.

Al-Ghazâlî, A.H. (1963). *Book XX of Al-Ghazâlî's Ihya Ulum Al-din*. Translated by L. Zolondek. Leiden: E.J. Brill.

Al-Ghazâlî, A.H. Cited in Scherer, G.H. (1933). *Al-Ghazâlî's Ayyuha 'L-Walad*, A Dissertation Submitted to the Graduate Faculty in Candidacy for the Degree of Doctor of Philosophy, Department of Old Testament Literature and Interpretation, The University of Chicago. Beirut, Syria: The American Press, pp. 51–77.

Ali, M.M. (2010). *The History and Philosophy of Islāmization of Knowledge*. Kuala Lumpur, Malaysia: IIUM Press.

Al-Talbi, A. (1993). Al-Fārābī (259–339 AH/872–950 AD). Thinkers on Education. *Prospects: The Quarterly Review of Comparative Education*. Paris, UNESCO: International Bureau of Education, 23(1/2), 353–372.

Ashraf, S.A. (1985). *New Horizons in Muslim Education*. Cambridge: Hodder & Stroughton.

Asmaa Mohd Arshad (2012). *KonsepTa'dib: TerasFalsafahPendidikan Islām. IAdabdan Peradaban: KaryaPengi'tirafanuntuk Syed Muhammad Naquib al-Attas*. Selangor: MPH Group Publishing.

Biesta, G.J.J. (2010). *Good Education in an Age of Measurement: Ethics, Politics, Democracy*. Boulder, CA: Paradigm Publishers.

Bocca-Aldaqre, F. (2019). How Can Education Be Islāmic? Al-Attas and Al-Farūqī's Frame Works in Contemporary Debate. *Journal of Education and Human Development*, 8(4), 49–53.

Principles of Islāmic psychology education 35

Cook, B.J. (n.d.) *History of Islāmic Education, Aims and Objectives of Islāmic Education*. The State University.com Education Encyclopaedia. https://education.stateuniversity.com/pages/2133/Islām.html (accessed 5 October 2022).

Gulzar, A.A. (2021). *The Influence of the World Conferences on Muslim Education*. https://educarepk.com/the-influence-of-the-world-conferences-on-muslim-education.html (accessed 2 October 2022).

Halstead, M. (2004). An Islāmic Concept of Education. *Comparative Education*, 40(4), 517–529.

Hassan, A., Suhid, A., Abiddin, N.Z., Ismail, H., & Hussin, H. (2010). The Role of Islāmic Philosophy of Education in Aspiring Holistic Learning. *Procedia – Social and Behavioral Sciences*, 5, 2113–2118.

Ibn Taymiyyah al-Ḥarrānī. *Majmoo Al-Fataawaa* 2/67–86, *Dar At-Tamaru* 1/10, *Ighaathatul Luhfaan* 2/372–373.

Ismail, S. (2020). *Al-Attas' Philosophy of Islāmic Education*. Conference Proceedings, ARICIS, Universitas Islām Negeri Ar-Raniry Banda Aceh, Indonesia, pp. 341–350.

Murris, K., & Verbeek, C. (2014). A Foundation for Foundation Phase Teacher Education: Making Wise Educational Judgements. *South African Journal of Childhood Education*, 4(2), 1–17.

Nasr, S.H. (1984). The Islāmic Philosophers' Views on Education. *Muslim Education Quarterly*, 2(4), 5–16.

Nata, A. (2013). Revitalisasi Pendidikan Karakter Untuk Mencetak Generasi Unggul. *Didaktika*, 1(1). http:// jurnal.iainkediri.ac.id/index.php/didaktika/article/view/114 (accessed 3 October 2022).

Rahman, T.A., Wan Sabri Wan, Y., Zuriati Mohd, R., & Amir, A.N. (2015). Al-Faruqi's Fundamental Ideas and Philosophy of Education. *Dinamika Ilmu*, 15(2), 235–247.

Rassool, G.H. (2020). Cognitive Restructuring of Psychology: The Case for A Vertical and Horizontal Integrated, Embedded Curriculum Model for Islāmic Psychology. *Islāmic Studies*, 59(4), 477–494.

Rassool, G.H. (2021). Decolonising Psychology and Its (dis) Contents. In G.H. Rassool (Ed.), *Islāmic Psychology: Human Behaviour and Experiences from an Islāmic Perspective*. Oxford: Routledge, pp. 583–601.

Rassool, G.H. (2022). *Foundation of Islāmic Psychology: From Classical Scholars to Contemporary Thinkers*. Oxford: Routledge.

Rayan, S. (2012). Islāmic Philosophy of Education. *International Journal of Humanities and Social Science*, 2(19), 150–156.

Siddique, F. (2012). Islāmic Education Pt 5: The Concept of Education in Islām – Analysis. www.Islām21c.com/Islāmic-thought/4561-Islāmic-education-pt-5-the-concept-of-education-in-Islām/ (accessed 17 September 2022).

3 Islāmisation of knowledge and knowledge integration

Introduction

The effects of colonisation, now replaced by globalisation, reduced the influence of Islāmic education to a lower-tier level in many colonised Muslim-majority countries. The imposition of an alien system of education significantly exposes Muslims to two parallel and contradictory systems of education: the Eurocentric and Orientalist system and the traditional Islāmic system (*Madrasahs* and *Ulūm*). This is reflected in the following statement by Husain and Ashraf (1979):

> This system of education imported into Muslim countries, fully subscribed to and supported by all governmental authorities, is one borrowed from the West. At the head of this system is the modem University, which is secular and hence non- in its approach to knowledge. Unfortunately, these people educated by this new system of education, known as modern education, are generally unaware of their own tradition and classical heritage. It is also not possible for this group to provide such leaderships we have envisaged.
>
> (pp. 16–17)

This duality produced not only "divided loyalties, confusion in the minds of students and intellectual schizophrenia of the *Ummah*'s educated elites" (Kasule, cited in Gulzar, 2021) but also double consciousness (the internal conflict experienced by subordinated or colonised groups in an oppressive society) (Du Bois, 1994). The philosophical foundation of the Eurocentric and Orientalist educational system is the antithesis of Islāmic beliefs and practices.

The colonial educational system is based on inculcating Western values, individualism, materialism, secularism and modernisation of social life, rationalistic in its quest for knowledge. Pluralism, the recognition and acceptance of diversity and cultural identity, had also been absent in the contents of the educational curriculum, as institutional racism is embedded in the colonial or globalised educational system. Secularism, as a deliberate institutional policy, also weakens and damages to the religio-cultural norms of the colonised societies. Cook (1999) suggests,

> Secularism, with its veneration of human reason over divine revelation and precepts of the separation of Mosque and state, is anathema to the Islāmic doctrine of *Tawhîd* (oneness), where all aspects of life whether spiritual or temporal are consolidated into a harmonious whole.
>
> (p. 340)

The secularisation of the educational system is also viewed as an essential component of the process of modernisation and is proposed as a universally valid imperative (El-Mesawi & Khriji, 2006). What is of interest here is that "by the turn of the twentieth century, most Muslim countries had newly created elites who had a vital interest in preserving and maintaining Western cultural traditions" (Cook, 1999, p. 340). It is within in this context that Islāmic scholars, revivalists, educators and reformers, including Jamaluddinn Afghani (1838–1897), Muhammad Abduh (1849–1905), Sheikh Al Hadi (1867–1934), Ashraf Ali Thanvi (1873–1943), Allamah Muhammad Iqbal (1879–1938), Sayyid Qutb (1906–1966), Syed Abul A'la Maududi (1903–1979), Al-Attas (1931–), Al-Farūqī (1921–1986), Abdul Hamid Ahmad AbuSulayman (1936–2021), M. K. Hassan (1942–), Seyyed Hossein Nasr (1933–) and many others, who were discontented with the nature of colonial education, made remarkable contributions and advancement of the "Islāmisation of knowledge" movement. This chapter aims to examine the concepts of Islāmisation of knowledge and knowledge integration. It proposes that the concept of "Islāmisation of knowledge" is not to be taken in the literal meaning of the term "Islāmisation," as it is used in everyday religious or political contexts.

Islāmisation of knowledge: an overview

In the context of this chapter, it is worth pointing out that the evolution of the process of the Islāmisation of psychology would not have gathered pace without the movement of the Islāmisation of knowledge (Al-Attas, 1978; Al-Faruqi, 1982; Rajab, 1999; Hashim & Rossid, 2000). The Islāmisation of knowledge is an intellectual movement that gained momentum in the 1970s, with the main purpose of Islāmising knowledge and the post-colonial educational system. This Islāmic revivalism was due to a number of factors, including

> the rise of the plight of the Muslim Ummah, the secularisation of the educational system in Muslim majority countries, the global reawakening of Islāmic consciousness, and the concern of Muslim scholars towards the adoption of Western-oriented values and life-styles by Muslims.
>
> (Rassool, 2021, p. 4)

Al-Attas (1978) proposes the concept of Islāmisation of knowledge and refers to it as "the liberation of man first from magical, mythological, animistic, national-cultural tradition, and then from secular control over his reason and his language" (p. 41). Al-Attas (1978) defines Islāmisation as "the liberation of man first from magical, mythological, animistic, national-cultural tradition, and then from secular control over his reason and his language" (p. 41). Al-Attas' (cited in Ali, 2010) reasoning was based on the following premises: "Western educational system is no longer relevant to the Muslim world as it is problematic, unjust, and brought chaos in man's life" (p. 112), and the problem with Western concept of knowledge is that it "creates confusion, scepticism, and it elevates doubt and speculation. To them, human reasoning is the true guide to man's success in life" (p. 119).

Al-Farūqī (1989, the doyen of the Islāmisation of knowledge, refers to Islāmisation as "a framework for human life, civilisation, and human transformation. It determines the purpose of every activity, struggle, action, and Islāmic social organization. It gave human life purpose and charts its course" (p. 87). He further adds,

> Islāmisation represent the truth, the justice, the transformation, and the reformation that concerns all Muslims. Its care and concern, by definition, extends to all human beings. It seeks to bestow dignity and honour upon all humans living on this earth. Islāmisation is the call that divinely based civilization has addressed to the present world which is torn apart with disaster looming large and clear.
>
> (p. 84)

Al-Farūqī held the belief that the process of Islāmisation should not be an individual activity but a collective one. That is, Islāmisation should be based on community obligation (*Fard Kifayah*) of the *Ummah* rather than individualistic venture. Al-Farūqī suggested that a university based on Islāmic ethics and traditional thoughts should be established, and the disciplines, including humanities and social and natural sciences, should be redesign and reformulated and integrated with Islāmic beliefs and practices.

In contrast, Hassan (2009) prefers the use of the concept of Islāmicisation rather than Islāmisation to provide an alternative to the secular knowledge of the Western and modern civilisation. Hassan (2013) argues that Islāmisation implies "the conversion of knowledge to Islām" and, in contrast, the term Islāmicisation "has a connotation of a process of conforming things to Islāmic principles or being in harmony with the teachings of Islām" (p. 43). The rationale for Islāmicisation include the following:

- Firstly, it denotes a process of conforming to Islām or being in harmony with the religion instead of being understood by others as a process of conversion to Islām.

Islāmisation of knowledge and knowledge integration 39

- Secondly, "Islāmicise" conveys a lot of meaning; some of them are "connected to Islām," "in agreement with Islāmic principles" and "complies with the teaching of Islām."
- Finally, the word conveys the idea of embracing something accepted by the religion's values and standards.

For A'la Mawdudi, the Islāmisation of knowledge focuses on a "critical analysis of western humanities and sciences to recast them in accordance with the teachings of Islām" (cited in Moten, 2004, p. 257). A'la Mawdudi asserts that

> Islām is not a "religion" in the sense this term is commonly understood. It is a system encompassing all fields of living. Islām means politics, economics, legislation, science, humanism, health, psychology, and sociology. It is a system which makes no discrimination on the basis of race, colour, language, or other external categories. Its appeal is to all mankind. It wants to reach the heart of every human being.
>
> (p. 191)

Sayed Hossein Nasr, a contemporary scholar, preferred the use of the term "Islāmic worldview" instead of the term "Islāmisation of knowledge." Yusuf (2015) maintains that Sayed Hossein Nasr based the Islāmisation of knowledge on the sacred science (*scientia sacra*) – that is, the knowledge that lies at the heart of divine revelations and traditional sciences. The Islāmisation of science, Sayed Hossein Nasr (2010a) argues,

> cannot but be the integration based upon criticism, assimilation and rejection of various elements of the existing sciences into the Islāmic intellectual universe and therefore another framework than the existing modern scientific paradigm, a framework in which *tawhid* reigns supreme and where every atom of the universe is seen to be created for a purpose and in accordance with the wisdom and plan of the Creator.

Concept of Islāmisation of knowledge

Dzilo (2012) maintains that the concept of Islāmisation of knowledge "is not monosemous but involves multiple approaches to the various forms of modern-world thought in the context of the Islāmic intellectual tradition, including metaphysical, epistemological, ethical and methodological premises regarding the modern issue of knowledge" (p. 247). The concept of Islāmisation of knowledge refers to the "recasting knowledge according to Islāmic tenets" (Al-Faruqi,1982, p. 48), the "integration of Islāmic revealed knowledge and the human sciences" (Rajab,1999, p. 33) or "fashion out an Islāmic paradigm of knowledge based on the Islāmic world view"(Yusuf, 2015, p. 69). Al-Faruqi (1989) states,

> It is necessary to Islāmise knowledge, i.e., to redefine and re-order data, rethink the reasoning and relate the data, to revaluate the conclusions, re-project the goals and to do so in such a way as to make the disciplines enrich the vision and serve the cause of Islām. To this end, the methodological categories of Islām – namely: the unity of truth, the unity of knowledge, the unity of humanity, the unity of life and purposeful character of creation, and the subservience of creation to man and of man to Allah – must replace the Western categories and determine the perception and ordering of reality.
>
> (p. 20)

Al-Farūqī (1989) characterises Islāmisation of knowledge as bridging the gap between religious and secular knowledge. He proposed the redesigning disciplines such as the humanities, social sciences and natural sciences on the foundation of the Islāmic worldview and principles of ethics and morality. He argues, "There can be no doubt that Islām is relevant to all aspects of thinking, of living, of being. This relevance must be articulated unmistakably in each discipline" (Al-Faruqi, 1989, p. 5). Yusuf (2015) argues that Islāmisation of knowledge

> is an attempt to fashion out an Islāmic paradigm of knowledge based on the Islāmic world view and its unique constitutive concepts and factors. This is because the knowledge as conceived in the West is value laden and has detached itself from *Tawhid* (unicity and sovereignty of God).
>
> (p .69)

Sulaiman (2000) refers to the Islāmisation of knowledge as "an attempt through which those aspects of the body and purpose of knowledge, and of the process and methodologies discovering, validating, imparting and applying it, which oppose Islām, are identified and made subservient to the Islāmic worldview" (p. 5). The application of Islāmisation of knowledge in the field of psychology means the integration of Islāmic sciences and ethics with scientific knowledge and evidenced-based practice, resulting in a psychology knowledge based on an Islāmic worldview. However, there is a word of caution from Malik Badri, the father of contemporary Islāmic psychology, that not all of Western psychology needs to be Islāmised. Badri (1979) comments

> We do not need to Islāmise psychophysics or the physiology of sight and hearing and the anatomy of the eye and ear. Nor do we need to Islāmise studies about the role of the brain neurotransmitter serotonin in our sleep behaviour and in adjusting our body clock, the role of the hormone

Islāmisation of knowledge and knowledge integration 41

noradrenalin in setting our energy level nor the influence of caffeine, alcohol or heroin on the human nervous system. We do not need to develop our own Islāmic statistical psychology or to raise an ethical battle against neutral theories of learning. Such areas, as I said are "no man's land" between psychology and other exact sciences.

(p. 9)

Despite the preference for a particular term, scholars shared a lot of commonalities with the same philosophy and essence in the explanation of Islāmisation of knowledge. The scholars share the same aim to change contemporary, secular knowledge so that the new produced knowledge is congruent with Islāmic beliefs and practices. The philosophy behind the Islāmisation of knowledge is to expose Muslims to *ijtihad* (independent reasoning), which is the renewal of and modernity in contemporary Islāmic thought in shaping educational policy and knowledge from an Islāmic epistemological perspective.

There have been many criticisms of the Islāmisation of knowledge. The criticisms are related to the term "Islāmisation of knowledge," which is regarded as being vague and confusing, and it is thought that *'ilm* (knowledge of truth) cannot be further Islāmised (Hassan, 2013). Haque (2018) suggests that the term "desecularisation of knowledge" should be used instead. He argues that there is no consensus among scholars on the definition and scope of Islāmisation.

Seyyed Vali Nasr (1991) called the Islāmisation of knowledge as a "burgeoning enterprise" which "is rooted in the reassertion of Muslim religious loyalties in the face of cataclysmic changes which have torn many Muslim societies asunder" (p. 387). He argues that the project "has mostly been shaped in the spirit of a political discourse than a level-headed academic undertaking. It was pioneered by the self-styled thinkers with no expertise in the field they were trying to revolutionise" (p. 387). Seyyed Vali Nasr contests that the appellation "Islāmisation" implicitly suggests that the subject under consideration has therefore been "unholy" and could be "sacralised" by the writ of the *Shari'ah* (p. 393). He proposes that the Islāmisation of knowledge

> does not purport to create the sciences or the social sciences anew, but to inform their outlook with Islāmic values. It is a process which begins in the *Shari'ah* but does not end with it. Islāmisation entails an intellectual revolution and not merely the implementation of religious laws. Finally, it should not begin with, rather end in, institutions and organizational expressions.
>
> (p. 399)

Sayed Hossein Nasr (1991) was also critical of the Islāmisation of knowledge because it was "pioneered by the self-styled thinkers with no expertise in the field they were trying to revolutionise" (p. 387). He prefers the use of the term "Islāmic worldview" (religious, rational and philosophical, it is all-encompassing and leads to oneness) instead of the term "Islāmisation of knowledge." In addition, Nasr (2010a) argues that Islāmisation of knowledge is based on focusing and depending only on a single component of the Islāmic tradition, which is the *Shari'ah* (Islāmic law), and neglecting the spiritual and intellectual tradition. Thus, it does not fully represent the Islāmisation process. He maintains that knowledge can be Islāmised if it is developed in a sacred framework based on the Tawhīdīc paradigm, metaphysical principles and basic moral values. As an alternative to the Islāmisation of knowledge, Nasr (2010b) presents some fundamental principles in shifting the paradigm of knowledge and suggests six major steps in his model that could be employed by those who are willing to engage in the process.

From Islāmisation of knowledge to knowledge integration

There is now a shift in terminology whereby the concept of knowledge integration has replaced Islāmisation of knowledge. Knowledge integration refers to "the process of merging two or more originally unrelated. knowledge structures into a single structure" (Schneider, 2012). Another version of knowledge integration is "the process of synthesising multiple knowledge models (or representations) into a common model (representation). knowledge integration focuses more on synthesizing the understanding of a given subject from different perspectives" (www.igi-global.com). Integration of knowledge is the process of synthesising the understanding of multiple knowledge disciplines into a common knowledge perspective. They include but are not limited to the integration of cultural, societal, theological and scientific perspectives of knowledge (cited in Sulaiman, 2016).

Carlile (2002) views knowledge integration as a bond of different specialist knowledge. In the context of this chapter, bonding different specialists' knowledge can also be understood as combining revealed knowledge and empirical knowledge. Knowledge integration can also be understood as a goal-directed process. Berggren et al. (2011) views knowledge integration as a combination of specialised knowledge in a goal-directed process, whereas Enberg (2007) refers to knowledge integration as a process of linking knowledge and claims it to be dynamic. Islāmic scholars have provided a diversity of definitions and explanations of knowledge integration. AbuSulayman (1994) refers to the integration of knowledge as a union between religious sciences and non-religious sciences. Sidek (2009) suggests that integration is a process of harmonisation between triadic concepts – Tawhīdic paradigm, values and human potential – in the educational system of contemporary Muslims. Kasule (2015) refers to the concept of knowledge integration as an evolutionary process that builds and adds value to existing knowledge. He suggests that "it involves integrating Islāmic moral and epistemological values in the various disciplines of knowledge that are taught" (p. 124). The themes of combining, sharing, synthesising and merging knowledge are a necessary condition for knowledge integration.

Knowledge integration can also be viewed as a kind of epistemological integration (*al-takamul al-ma'rifi*) (Malkawi, 2014). Malkawi states that epistemological integration

> might be classified, for example, as a branch of philosophy-ontology, epistemology, or ethics-in which case it takes on an abstract, theoretical dimension. It might also be classified as a type of cultural, social activity when the purpose for which it is undertaken is to provide necessary resources and to transform them into political, economic or social activity in order to facilitate life for people on the practical level, in which case it takes on a social, applied dimension.
>
> (2014, p. 4)

He also points to the application of epistemological integration of diverse but related field of knowledge in designing curriculum programmes. Thus, knowledge integration in psychology knowledge is the synthesis of revealed knowledge and empirical knowledge, as well as the transfer of knowledge in teaching practices. Initially, the task is to produce a curriculum that will deliver integrated knowledge of Islāmic sciences and worldview with classical and contemporary knowledge of psychology. Both evidenced-based psychological knowledge and Islāmic intellectual tradition are maintained with adherence to the demands of any prescribed national curriculum. The idea of transformation of integrated knowledge during teaching practices allows us to view knowledge integration as a processual phenomenon. Hence, the process of knowledge integration itself can be interpreted as a process of exchanging integrated knowledge between the teacher and the student. For psychology, the process of desecularisation has begun and efforts are being made to reconstruct psychology based on an Islāmic epistemological paradigm (Rassool, 2021).

Conclusion

The inferences that can be made from the presented explanation of the concept of Islāmisation of knowledge and knowledge integration indicate a paradigm shift in the contents of knowledge and reject the notion of a reductionist and secular knowledge that is incongruent with Islāmic thought and epistemology. Knowledge integration has a duality of purpose. Willem et al. (2008) consider knowledge integration to be a transfer of knowledge as well as its application. As we have examined Islāmisation of knowledge and knowledge integration, we see issues and challenges in the process of knowledge integration. One of the key issues in knowledge integration lies in the lack of preparation of lectures in implementing knowledge integration, resulting in role adequacy, role legitimacy and role conflict. Another issue involved is the abilities of lecturers to access the relevant and appropriate knowledge and utilise available resources and then integrate this knowledge efficiently and flexibly. The diversity of lecturers in relations to their level of tacit knowledge area of Islāmic studies will also inhibit the implementation of integration both in the curriculum and in teaching practices. The issues of cultural resistance, negative attitudes towards innovation, lack of support from competent authority and organisational structures may also have varying implications on the effectiveness of implementing and transferring knowledge integration.

Bibliography

AbuSulayman, A.H. (1994). *Islāmization of Knowledge: Reforming Contemporary Knowledge*. VA: USA: International Institute of Islāmic Thought.
Al-Attas, S.M.N. (1978). *Islām and Secularism*. Kuala Lumpur: ABIM.
Al-Farūqi, I.R. (1982). *Islāmization of Knowledge: Problems, Principles and Prospective*. Proceedings & Selected Papers of the Second Conference on Islāmization of Knowledge, 1402 AH /1982 AD. Herndon, V: IIIT.
Al-Farūqi, I.R. (1989). *Islāmisation of Knowledge-General Principles and Work Plan*. Herndon, VA: International Institute of Islāmic Thought.
Ali, M.M. (2010). *The History and Philosophy of Islāmization of Knowledge*. Kuala Lumpur, Malaysia: IIUM Press.
Al Migdadi, M.H. (2011). Issues in Islāmization of Knowledge, Man and Education. *Revue Académique des Sciences Humaines et Sociales*, 7, 11.
Badri, M.B. (1979). *The Dilemma of Muslim Psychologists*. London: MWH.
Berggren, C., Bergek, A., Bengtsson, L., & Söderlund, J. (2011). Knowledge Integration and Innovation. In C. Berggren, A. Bergek, L. Bengtsson, M. Hobday, & J. Söderlund (Eds.), *Knowledge Integration and Innovation: Critical Challenges Facing International Technology-Based Firms*. New York: Oxford University Press.
Biesta, G.J.J. (2010). *Good Education in an Age of Measurement: Ethics, Politics, Democracy*. Boulder, CA: Paradigm Publishers.
Boostrom, R. (2010). Hidden Curriculum. In C. Kridel (Ed.), *Encyclopaedia of Curriculum Studies*. Los Angeles: SAGE, pp. 440–441.
Carlile, P. (2002). A Pragmatic View of Knowledge and Boundaries: Boundary Objects in New Product Development. *Organization Science*, 13(4), 422–455.
Cook, B.J. (1999). Islāmic Versus Western Conceptions of Education: Reflections on Egypt. *International Review of Education/Internationale Zeitschrift für Erziehungswissenschaft/Revue Internationale de l'Education*, 45(3/4), 339–357.
Du Bois, W.E.B. (1994). *The Souls of Black Folk*. New York, Avenel, NJ: Gramercy Books.
Dzilo, H. (2012). The Concept of "Islāmization of Knowledge" and its Philosophical Implications. *Islām and Christian – Muslim Relations*, 23(3), 247–256.
El-Mesawi, M. El-Tahir, & Khriji, T. (2006). Islām and Terrorism: Beyond the Wisdom of the Secularist Religion. *Intellectual Discourse*, 14(1), 47–70.
Enberg, C. (2007). *Projects Knowledge Integration in Product Development*. Doctoral thesis. Department of Management and Engineering, Linköping University, Sweden.

Islāmisation of knowledge and knowledge integration 45

Gulzar, A.A. (2021). *The Influence of the World Conferences on Muslim Education.* https://educarepk.com/the-influence-of-the-world-conferences-on-muslim-education.html (accessed 18 September 2022).

Haque, A. (2018). *Islāmization of Knowledge: The Case of Psychology.* Department of Islāmic Studies. Aligarh Muslim University.

Hashim, R., & Rossid, I. (2000). Islāmization of Knowledge: A Comparative Analysis of the Conceptions of Al-Attas and Al-Faruqi. *Intellectual Discourse,* 8(1), 19–44.

Hassan, M.K. (2009). Islāmization of Human Knowledge: Why and What? Cited in Rashid, M.S.B.A., & Manaf, A.M.A. (2014). *Islāmization of Human Knowledge: A Critical Analysis.* COMM 6030: Issues and Methodologies: Islāmization of Communication. International Islāmic University of Malaysia.

Hassan, M.K. (2013). *Islāmisation of Human Knowledge as the Most Important Mission of IIUM.* Unpublished paper. Kuala Lumpur: International Islāmic University, Malaysia (IIUM).

Husain, S.S., & Ashraf, S.A. (1979). *Crisis in Muslim Education.* Jeddah: Hodder and Stoughton.

Kasule, O.H. (2015). Integration of Knowledge (IOK) and Textbook Writing for Islāmic Universities. *International Journal of Islāmic Thought,* 4(1), 123–126.

Malkawi, F.H. (2014). *Epistemological Integration: Essentials of an Islamic methodology.*). Herndon, VA: The International Institute of Islamic Thought.

Moten, A.R. (2004). Islāmization of Knowledge in Theory and Practice. *Islāmic Studies,* 43(2), 247–272.

Murris, K., & Verbeek, C. (2014). A Foundation for Foundation Phase Teacher Education: Making Wise Educational Judgements. *South African Journal of Childhood Education,* 4(2), 1–17.

Nasr, S.H. (1989). *Knowledge and the Sacred.* New York: State University of New York Press.

Nasr, S.H. (2010a), Islām and the Problem of Modern Science. *Islām and Science,* 8(1), 63–74. Cited in The Free Library. (2014). Retrieved May 17 2023 from https://www.thefreelibrary.com/Islam+and+the+problem+of+modern+science.-a0230685062.

Nasr, H. S. (2010b). *Islāmic Life and Thought.* Kuala Lumpur: Islāmic book Trust.

Nasr, V. (1991). Islāmization of Knowledge: A Critical Overview. *Islāmic Studies,* 30(3), 387–400.

Ragab, I.A. (1995). On the Nature and Scope of the Islāmization Process: Towards Conceptual Clarification. *Intellectual Discourse,* 3(2), 113–122.

Rajab, I.A. (1999). On the Methodology of Islāmizing the Social Sciences. *Intellectual Discourse,* 7(1), 27–52.

Rassool, G.H. (2020). Cognitive Restructuring of Psychology: The Case for A Vertical and Horizontal Integrated, Embedded Curriculum Model for Islāmic Psychology. *Islāmic Studies,* 59(4), 477–494.

Rassool, G.H. (2021a). *Islāmic Psychology: Human Behaviour and Experience from an Islāmic Perspective.* Oxford: Routledge.

Rassool, G.H. (2021b). Decolonising Psychology and its (Dis) Contents. In G.H. Rassool (Ed.), *Islāmic Psychology: Human Behaviour and Experiences from an Islāmic Perspective.* Oxford: Routledge, pp. 583–601.

Schneider, M. (2012). Knowledge Integration. In N.M. Seel (Ed.), *Encyclopedia of the Sciences of Learning.* Boston, MA: Springer. https://doi.org/10.1007/978-1-4419-1428-6_807.

Sidek, B. (2009). The Integrated Approach in Malaysian Education: The International Islāmic University as a Model. *Journal Pedidikan Islām*, 13(2), 87–99.

Sulaiman, S. (2000). *The Islāmization of Knowledge: Background, Models and Way Forward*. Kano, Nigeria: The International Institute of Islāmic Thought.

Sulaiman, S. (2016). *Islāmization of Knowledge and Integration of Knowledge: A Conceptual Clarification*. www.academia.edu/30341820/ISLĀMIZATION_OF_KNOWLEDGE_AND_INTEGRATION_OF_KNOWLEDGE_A_CONCEPTUAL_CLARIFICATION (accessed 21 September 2022).

Willem, A., Scarbough, H., & Beulens, M. (2008). Impact of Coherent Versus Multiple Identities on Knowledge Integration. *Journal of Information Science*, 34(3), 370–386.

www.igi-global.com. *Knowledge Integration*. www.igi-global.com/infosci-ondemand/search/?p=knowledge%20integration&pg=1 (accessed 21 September 2022).

Yusuf, Y.M. (2015). Seyyed Hossein Nasr on Islāmisation of Knowledge. *International Journal of Islāmic Thoughts*, 4(2), 69–78.

4 Curriculum design and development

Introduction and context

There is a diversity of definitions and explanations of what is a curriculum. The term is highly contextual and implies different political, social and ideological meanings dependent upon on the way it is used (Ewing, 2013). The term in its simplicity is regarded as "planned learning experiences" (Johnson, 1967, p. 129). A more comprehensive definition of the curriculum is "The planned and guided learning experiences and intended outcomes, formulated through the systematic reconstruction of knowledge and experience, under the auspices of the school, for the learner's continuous and willful growth in person-social competence" (Tanner & Tanner, 1975, p. 13). In higher academic institutions, the term is used in different way: the structure and content of a unit (subject), the structure and content of a programme of study, the students' experience of learning, and dynamic and interactive process of teaching and learning (Fraser & Bosanquet, 2006). Due to the diversity in the meaning of the term, Lattuca and Stark (2009) advocate the use of an "academic plan," which focuses on the planning process. The terms "curriculum design" and "curriculum development" are used interchangeably. Curriculum design is described as "the purposeful, deliberate, and systematic organisation of curriculum (instructional blocks) within a class or course" (Schweitzer, 2020). In a similar vein, curriculum development is described as "encompassing how a curriculum is planned, implemented, and evaluated" (Ornstein & Hunkins, 2009, p. 17).

This means that the curriculum is designed and developed for a specific educational programme that define the teaching and learning activities, assessment programme for the benefit of the students in their development in the acquisition of knowledge, and the development of skills and attitudes. In addition, learning resources are identified to support the effective delivery of the course. In order to design a curriculum for a course in Islāmic psychology, it is essential to adopt a particular model of curriculum development. To this end, the integrated curriculum is the most appropriate model for the knowledge synthesis of psychology with Islāmic studies, Islāmic ethics and Islāmic psychology. The goal of integration is to produce a curriculum of psychology

DOI: 10.4324/9781003329596-4

48 Curriculum design and development

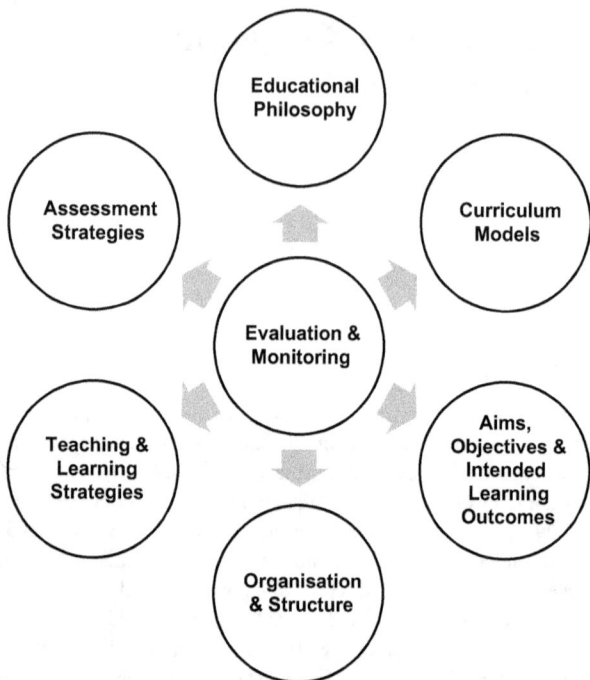

Figure 4.1 A map of curriculum design and development

from an Islāmic perspective. This chapter examines the nature and process of curriculum design and development and explores some of the curriculum models used in higher education. Figure 4.1 presents a map of curriculum design and development.

Educational philosophy development

Having gathered evidence for the need in the deconstruction of the psychology curriculum, the development of an educational philosophy, referred to as a "vision and values statement" (Stark, 2000; O'Neill, 2010), is a necessity. For example, Riphah International University in Pakistan the mission statement is the "Establishment of state-of-the-art educational institutions with a focus on inculcating Islāmic ethical values." The Islāmic ethical values are *Muhasabah* (accountability), *Ijtimaiyyah* (teamwork), *Mushawarah* (consultation and harmony), *Rahmah* (compassion), *Itqan* (pursuits of excellence), and *Al-Akhirah* (*Akhirah*-oriented decisions). The values and vision communicate the fundamental basis of the type of education provided and define a clear sense of direction of how to design and develop the educational programmes.

Course programmes also need an educational philosophy that is more specific to the nature and contents of the educational programme. An example of the undergraduate BS or BA in psychology.

This programme aims to educate students in a systematic, scientific study about human behaviours and experiences from both secular and Islāmic perspectives. In addition, the programme aims to develop the students' clinical skills to enable them apply the knowledge and skills in real-world application, and for further training in academic psychology and research or pursue careers in a number of areas of employment. We value and therefore encourage our students to adhere to the mission and values of Riphah International University and be reflective. We aim to provide a learning environment that will enable students to grow and develop on a personal and professional level.

Curriculum models

Having formulated an educational philosophy for the programme, the next stage is to identify the curriculum model or combination of models that would suit the entire or certain aspects of the programme. Curriculum model is a framework that guides designers to map out the rationale for the contents, and the teaching and learning activities. There have been numerous authors who have attempted to encapsulate the nature of curriculum, which reflected their own philosophies and ideologies. A simplistic and polarised versions of curriculum models are those referred to by many authors as the product model and the process model. The models have different emphases: plans and intentions (product model) and activities and effects (process model) (Neary, 2003, p. 39) (see Figure 4.2). In most modern curriculum designs, there is an element of both these models.

The product model can be traced to the writings of Bobbitt (1918), who was the pioneer in the behavioural objectives approach to curriculum planning. Among the curriculum theorists in the product model include Tyler (1949), Bloom (1956), Gagne (1967), Popham and Baker (1970) and Rowntree (1974). According to Tyler (1949), behavioural objectives provide the foundations on which product models of the curriculum are built. Rowntree (1974), for example, argues that the use of behavioural objectives facilitates the intention of the teaching and learning activities and therefore leads to more purposeful learning. Rowntree further argues that behavioural objectives enable the selection of structure and content of teaching, leading to more accurate methods of assessment and evaluation. One of the value-added contributions of the product model in the curriculum is the application of is

50 Curriculum design and development

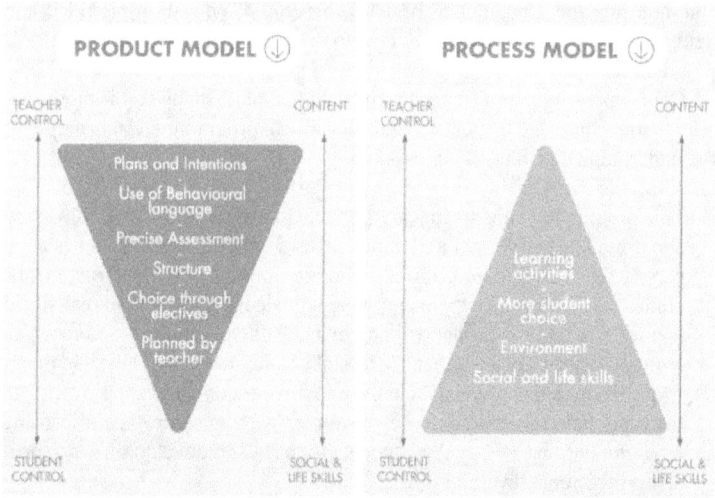

Figure 4.2 Product and process models
Source: O'Neill (2015) (with kind permission)

Bloom's taxonomy of educational objectives (Bloom, 1969). These taxonomies, which include the cognitive, affective and psychomotor domains, are now the pillars of curriculum planning.

One of the early critics of behavioural objectives was Eisner (1967), who argues that despite its rational approach, some creative courses do not lend themselves to behavioural specificity. For example, ethics and moral values cannot be included in measurable behavioural objectives. It is difficult to judge what the impact of particular learning experiences has been. When there is too much focus on behavioural outcomes, Schubert (1986) agrees that outcomes resulting from the hidden curriculum and the culture of schooling are emphasised, while important aspects are overlooked. Some critics of the objective approach argue that this process turns "educators into technicians" and is "teacher proof" (Smith, 2000), is a "threat to individual freedom" (Kelly, 1999) and lacks a procedure between integrating learning experience content and evaluation (Huang & Yang, 2004). However, despite its limitations, the product model "has been valuable in developing and communicating transparent outcomes to the student population and has moved emphasis away from lists of content" (O'Neill, 2015, p. 27).

An alternative approach of looking at curriculum theory and practice is the process model. Stenhouse (1975) views the curriculum as a process and maintains, "As a minimum, a curriculum should provide a basis for planning a course, studying it empirically and considering the grounds of its justification" (p. 5). This process model is also considered as "an organic process by which learning is offered, accepted and internalized" (Newman & Ingram, 1989, p. 1). Some of the characteristics of the process model include using open-ended objectives or learning outcomes, having a holistic approach regarding human potential as a unity, active learning and student-centredness, attention shifts from teaching to learning, promoting critical thinking and enabling reflective practices. The promotion and enabling of critical thinking is reflected in the following statement: "It is a way of translating any educational idea into a hypothesis testable in practice. It invites critical testing rather than acceptance" (Stenhouse, 1975, p. 142). The essence of this type of learning activities is the development of understanding rather than the acquisition of knowledge (Kelly, 1999, p. 78). This suggests that when working with learning outcomes that lean more toward product model, it may be more valuable to first consider the contents and teaching/learning activities and to then write the learning outcomes.

In addition to the process and product models, there are a range of different, more specific, models that may be appropriate for your course design and development. There is the backward design (Wiggins & McTighe, 2010), cognitive thought model (Lakoff & Núñez, 2000), the deliberative model (Ornstein & Hunkins, 2004), the post-positivism models (Ornstein & Hunkins, 2004) and the experiential and social critical models (Toohey, 2000). To increase our understanding of these models, it is worth examining the subject-centred or learner-centred models (described as "designs" by Ornstein & Hunkins, 2004). Subject-centred designs are based on the notion of a discipline-based programme merging with other disciplines into an interdisciplinary subject area (correlation and integration of knowledge) and based on culture and experiences. In contrast, learner-centred designs are negotiated designs (use of learning contract) between students and teachers, involving what the students would like to or need to learn. Emphasis is on the process of learning, not on the content, and integration of knowledge is encouraged.

This is an overview of different models in current use in higher education. No one model is ideal, and no one model may suit a full programme. The models that are appropriate for knowledge integration is a combination of the product and process models (including experiential learning) depending on the sub-disciplines of psychology and the subject matter of Islāmic studies, Islāmic ethics and Islāmic psychology. Ornstein and Hunkins (2009) suggest that although curriculum development models are technically useful, they often overlook the human aspects, such as the personal attitudes, feelings and values involved in curriculum making. Curriculum designers need to seek the appropriate models for knowledge and curriculum integration to become a reality.

Aims, learning objectives and intended learning outcomes

Following the design wheel, the next stage is the development of programme aims and/or learning objectives and intended learning outcomes to assist curriculum design and development. Aims are general statements of intent of a programme, a module or even an individual lecture or seminar. Aims provide a sense of direction of learning (for the student) and teaching (for the teacher). There is the suggestion that aims are concerned with teaching and the teacher's intentions, whilst learning outcomes are concerned with learning (Adam, 2004). Moon (2002) suggests that aims indicate the general content, direction and intention behind the programme from the designer/ teacher viewpoint.

When defining learning aims, it can be helpful to ask questions such as:

- From your perspective as the educator, what is this piece of learning for?
- What are the main benefits it will bestow on learners?
- What is the programme or module trying to achieve?

(Imperial College London)

Some well-defined learning aims are as follows:

- The aims of the course are to provide the students with in-depth knowledge of Islāmic psychology and ethics and the application of Islāmic psychotherapy with a strong research focus.
- The programme aims to equip the students to work as a psychotherapist/ counsellor, be cognisant with spiritual interventions and make independent clinical decisions in a variety of settings based on an Islāmic perspective. It offers an opportunity to critically and creatively evaluate current approaches and practice issues of psychotherapy and counselling that are congruent with Islāmic ethics.
- This module will provide a general overview of the integrated research methods in Islāmic psychology and reinforce understanding of the importance of integrated research for the evaluation of psychotherapeutic outcomes.
- The aim of the module is to examine the historical, philosophical and theological paradigm of Islāmic psychology and psychotherapy from classical to contemporary scholars.

The writing of the learning objectives of a programme, module or class is another important aspect of curriculum design and development. It is important to note that learning objectives are not a substitute for the student-focused intended learning outcomes. These terms are used interchangeably, but there are some important differences. Learning objectives are statements, written

Curriculum design and development

from the perspective of the teacher, about how aims are to be achieved (what does the teacher want to accomplish?).

Questions that are useful for guiding the development of learning objectives might include:

- What teaching methods will be used?
- What are students going to be doing? What kinds of learning activities will they engage in?
- What new knowledge, skills or understanding do you intend learners to gain, and at what level?

(Imperial College London)

Here are some examples of learning objectives of a module on Islāmic ethics and psychotherapy.

The learning objectives of this module are to accomplish the following:

- To stress the importance of the professional code of ethics and practice in psychotherapy and counselling
- To examine the issues related to confidentiality and informed consent in the Islāmic context
- To develop awareness of ethical issues and dilemmas in the psychotherapy relationship
- To develop a sound knowledge and understanding of the legal issues relevant to psychotherapy practice
- To introduce issues arising from having dual or multiple roles as an Islāmic psychotherapist

Learning aims are described as general statements of intent for the programme or module and learning objectives describing what the teacher wants to accomplish or how the teacher intends to facilitate the achievement of those aims. Intended learning outcomes (ILOs) are seen more from the learner's perspective (what will the student need to learn in this module or programme?). ILOs are

> concise statements of how learners will demonstrate that they have achieved the intended learning at the end of a programme or module. They describe what learners will be expected to be able to do if they have been successful, and they indicate the appropriate level of learner achievement.

(Imperial College London)

ILOs are written in the SMART format – that is, specific, measurable, achievable, realistic and time-bound. ILOs focus on the demonstration of knowledge, skills and attitudes, and they need to be constructively aligned with both the learning activities and with the methods of assessment.

54 Curriculum design and development

Upon successful completion of this module, students will be able to do the following:

- Identify the different approaches and models of psychotherapy based on the Western tradition
- Discuss some of the models of Islāmic counselling and psychotherapy and their strengths and limitations
- Identify some of the barriers that make Muslims reluctant to access psychotherapy and counselling services
- List the stages in Rassool's Islāmic psychotherapy practice model
- Discuss the stages in Rassool's Islāmic psychotherapy practice model
- Discuss the strengths and limitations of this model
- Apply the stages of Rassool's Islāmic psychotherapy practice model in clinical interventions

ILOs are closely related to learning objectives because a trainer's objectives will ultimately be translated into ILOs. To write effective ILOs, it will be useful to examine key aspects of Bloom's taxonomy (Anderson & Krathwohl, 2001), a classification framework that supports and sometimes informs the design of ILOs. Bloom's taxonomy's of educational objectives is based on three domains:

- The cognitive domain – the knowledge-based domain, consisting of six levels (knowledge, comprehension, application, analysis, synthesis and evaluation)
- The affective domain – the attitudinal-based domain, consisting of five levels (receiving, responding, valuing, organisation and characterisation by value set)
- The psychomotor domain – the skill-based domain, consisting of six levels (reflex movements, basic fundamental movements, perceptual movements, physical activities, skilled movements and non-discursive communication)

The taxonomy for the cognitive, affective and psychomotor domains is often represented in the form of a pyramid and is a useful tool to guide the development of assignments, assessments and overall curricula. The taxonomy explains that (1) before you can understand a concept, you need to remember it; (2) to apply a concept, you need to first understand it; (3) to evaluate a process, you need to first analyse it; (4) to create something new, you need to have completed a thorough evaluation (Shabatura, 2013).

Programme organisation and structure

It is important at this stage to examine the relationship of the course or module's components in order to address the challenge of coherence in curriculum organisation. Bearn et al. (2008) describe the curriculum structure "like the

Table 4.1 Coherence in curriculum organisation

	Contents	Questions
Scope	Breadth and the depth of content Content: knowledge, affective (values and attitudes) and psychomotor (motor) skills Associated with horizontal integration curriculum design	"What does the teacher cover?" versus "What does the student seek out and do?"
Sequence	Focuses on the order in which things occur Logical development • Simple to complex learning • Prerequisite learning • Whole to part (inquiry/problem-based concept) • Chronological learning (historical/developmental)	Which order will the subject matter or themes de developed?
Continuity	Associated with the vertical integration curriculum design Revisit knowledge and skills in more depth as they progress Continuity relates to the subject matter but also to other skills, such as teamwork and problem-solving.	How do you address the continuity in an education programme?
Integration	Making links within a curriculum Connecting skills and knowledge from multiple sources and experiences Applying theory to practice Utilising diverse and even contradictory points of view Knowledge integration is linked to the idea of continuity.	What is the scope and level of integration?
Articulation	Articulate the horizontal and vertical relationship of a programme Use of mapping tools	How do you articulate the horizontal and vertical relationships of a programme to the various stakeholders?
Balance	Balance the discipline knowledge with other more generic skills	What do you need to do to balance the discipline of knowledge?

Source: Adapted from O'Neill (2010)

skeleton of a body: strong and in balance, giving direction and support to activities and determining the outline of what it represents. It needs careful consideration and planning" (p. 77). Ornstein and Hunkins (2009) have suggested that that attention should be given to the curriculum's scope, sequence, continuity, integration, articulation and balance (pp. 186–190). Table 4.1 provides an overview of the factors in the provision of coherence in curriculum organisation.

Ornstein and Hunkins (2009) suggest that the programme team should do the following:

- Reflect on the educational philosophy and the curriculum models of the programme (Do you/your team believe basic concepts must be done first?)
- Consider the students' needs (Do students see relevance of materials in first year? Are they straight from school or a more mixed group?)
- Sketch out the various designs (What are the relationships and good overlaps?)
- Cross-check with aims/outcomes/learning experiences/evaluation
- Share design with others

Teaching and learning strategies

The teaching and learning strategies would be dependent on the educational philosophy of the programme. If this educational philosophy is based on problem-solving or experiential learning, this should be reflected and transparent in the programme's teaching and learning strategies. The educational philosophy, the model of education and the intended learning outcomes would enable constructive alignment with the teaching and learning strategies. Bigg (2014) and Biggs and Tang (2011) suggest that in constructive alignment, there is the initial start with the outcomes the students to learn and align teaching and assessment to those outcomes. The trends in teaching and learning activities include "Engagement and empowerment of students in the curriculum; Social dimension of learning, including communities of practice, peer learning; Experiential and work-based learning; Approaches to encourage creativity and innovation; Internationalisation of the curriculum; and Increasing blended and online learning" (O'Neill, 2010, p. 71).

Programme assessment strategies

There is a need to have a further constructive alignment between the intended learning outcomes, learning and teaching activities and assessment methods. This constructive alignment is illustrated in Figure 4.3

Assessing student learning across a programme is part of the process of curriculum design and development. Assessment plays a key role in relation to the structure of the programme. Assessment has an important "gatekeeper" role by ensuring that the student has the required the necessary professional knowledge and competence required by professional and statutory bodies. In addition to the evaluation of the students' academic and clinical progress, assessment also contribute to improve student learning (formative assessment), to provide certification (summative assessment) and to contribute to quality assurance (Bloxham & Boyd, 2008).

Curriculum design and development 57

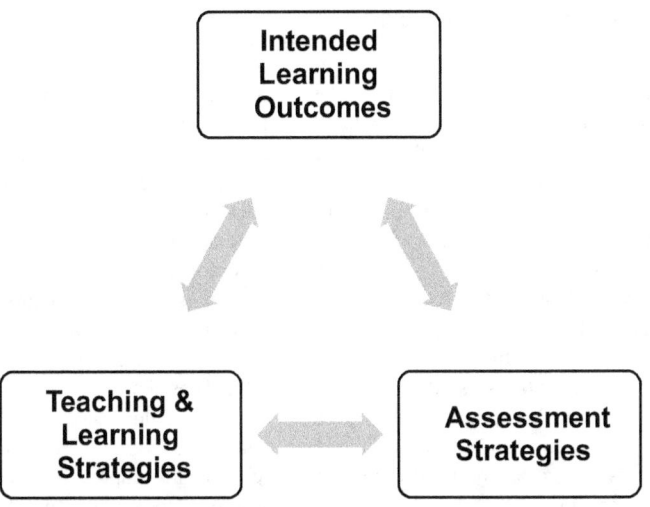

Figure 4.3 Constructive alignment

There is a need to have both formative and summative assessments, which are an essential part of any curriculum map. Formative assessments are informal assessments that evaluate a student's learning progress. Formative assessment refers to an assessment that is specifically intended to generate feedback on performance to improve and accelerate learning (Sadler, 2010). The purpose of formative assessment is to monitor student learning and provide ongoing feedback to teachers and students. In this way, by having feedback, it enables students to identify their strengths and weaknesses in a particular area of study. The forms of formative assessment may include teacher assignment, peer feedback or self-assessment. There is no formal grading as the assessment has no effect on the formal overall grading at the end of the course. In contrast, summative assessments are formal assignments that evaluate how the academic or clinical progress of the student, and they have high stakes. The purpose of summative assessment, based on some standard or benchmark, is to evaluate student learning at the end of a programme or module. The content and methodology of assessment must be within the boundaries of the intended learning outcomes and competences. There must be a balance between formative and summative assessments for an effective assessment strategy. Balancing assessment, it is argued, is a key aspect of an integrative approach to enhancing assessment (UK Quality Assurance Agency for Higher Education, 2007). An over-reliance on any type of assessment may be counterproductive in the learning process.

Evaluation and monitoring

Evaluation and monitoring are an ongoing process in curriculum design and development not a tail-end process, as illustrated in Figure 4.1. Evaluating individual modules or courses is vitally important as they allow the curriculum planners to identify the strengths and limitations of the programmes, to hear what students think about the programmes, to identify good practice and to improve the teaching and learning strategies. Evaluation is undertaken throughout the process of curriculum design and development. In addition, it enables decision-making at various stages of curriculum development. For course facilitators, it provides a mechanism for reflection on their course, to consider the impact of any changes made in previous years or what changes could be made in future years to improve their course. The design of the curriculum should be assessed periodically and refined based on assessment data. This may involve making minor alterations to the curriculum design. According to Scriven (1967), there are the three main types: formative evaluation (occurs during the course of curriculum development to improve the educational programme), summative evaluation (the effectiveness of the curriculum is evaluated on the basis of its stated aims during the process of its development) and diagnostic evaluation (evaluation of intended learning outcomes, formative assessment).

There are some common core principles when considering evaluation of face-to-face programmes. The feedback process will involve students, teachers, supervisors, external lecturers and administrative program personnel. The multi-mode of evaluative methods will include questionnaires, group discussions, interviews, focus groups, peer (colleague) evaluation, self-evaluation and self-reflection. This increases the reliability and validity of the evaluation process. The evaluation will involve a number of strategies from traditional statistical methods to illuminative approaches and will cover a variety of component:

- Analysis of teaching and learning resources
- Attitudes of students
- Student course feedback form
- Assessment of the aims of the programme
- Achievement of intended learning outcomes
- Organisation problems
- Analysis of costs
- Unintended outcomes

However, it has been suggested, "There are broader considerations for evaluation at institutional level, for example: institutional costs and investment in the programme; technology; staff time; choice of technology; staff training needs; student access and inclusion; ethical issues; pedagogical models; copyright, etc." (O'Neill, 2010, p. 101). Mainly, the curriculum monitoring and evaluation will meet the academic and professional requirements of different stakeholders, internal and external to the institution

Bibliography

Adam, S. (2004). *Using Learning Outcomes: A Consideration of the Nature, Role, Application and Implications for European Education of Employing "Learning Outcomes" at the Local, National and International Levels.* United Kingdom Bologna Seminar 1–2 July 2004, Heriot-Watt University (Edinburgh Conference Centre) Edinburgh, Scotland.

Anderson, L.W., & Krathwohl, D.R. (2001). *A Taxonomy for Learning, Teaching, and Assessing: A Revision of Bloom's Taxonomy of Educational Objectives.* New York: Longman.

Bearn, D., Cema, I., Dummer, P.M.H., et al. (2008). Curriculum Structure: Principles and Strategy. *European Journal of Dental Education,* 12(Suppl. 1), 74–84.

Biggs, J. (2014). Constructive alignment in university teaching. *HERDSA Review of Higher Education,* 1, 5–22.

Biggs, J., & Tang, C. (2011). *Teaching for Quality Learning at University.* Buckingham: Open University Press/McGraw Hill.

Bloom, B.S. (1956). *Taxonomy of educational objectives. Vol. 1: Cognitive domain.* New York: McKay, 20, 24.

Bloom, B.S. (1969). *Taxonomy of Educational Objectives: The Classification of Educational Goals.* Boston: Addison-Wesley Longman Ltd.

Bloxham, S., & Boyd, P. (2008). *Developing Effective Assessment in Higher Education: A Practical Guide.* Maidenhead: Open University Press McGraw-Hill.

Bobbitt, F. (1918). *The Curriculum.* Boston, MA: Houghton Mifflin.

Bruner, J. (1972). *The Relevance of Education.* London: Allen & Unwin.

Eisner, E.W. (1967). Educational Objectives: Help or Hindrance? *School Review,* 75, 250–266.

Ewing, R. (2013). *Curriculum and Assessment: Storylines.* Melbourne: Oxford University Press.

Fraser, S., & Bosanquet, A. (2006). The Curriculum? That's Just a Unit Outline, Isn't It? *Studies in Higher Education,* 31, 269–284.

Gagne, R.M. (1967). Curriculum Research and the Promotion of Learning. In R.E. Stake (Ed.), *Perspectives of Curriculum Evaluation.* Chicago: Rand McNally.

Huang, G.H., & Yang, L.L. (2004). *Curriculum Development and Design: Concept and Practice.* Taipei: Hsi Ta Shu Yuan.

Imperial College London. *Aims, Objectives, Outcomes – What's the Difference?* Education Development Unit. www.imperial.ac.uk/staff/educational-development/teaching-toolkit/intended-learning-outcomes/aims-objectives-outcomes-whats-the-difference/ (accessed 29 September 2022).

Johnson, M. (1967). Definitions and Models in Curriculum Theory. *Educational Theory,* 17(2), 127–140.

Kelly, A.V. (1999). *The Curriculum Theory and Practice* (4th ed.). Thousand Oaks, CA: Sage Publications Inc.

Lakoff, G., & Núñez, R.E. (2000). *Where Mathematics Comes From. How the Embodied Mind Brings Mathematics into Being.* New York: Basic Books.

Lattuca, L.R., & Stark, J.S. (2009). *Shaping the College Curriculum: Academic Plans in Context* (2nd ed.). San Francisco, CA: Jossey-Bass Inc.

Moon, J. (2002). *The Module and Programmes Development Handbook.* London: Kogan Page.

Neary, M. (2003). *Curriculum Concepts and Research: Curriculum Studies in Post-Compulsory and Adult Education: A Teacher's and Student Teacher's Study Guide*. Cheltenham: Nelson Thornes Ltd.

Newman, E., & Ingram, G. (1989). *The Youth Work Curriculum*. London: Further Education Unit (FEU).

O'Neill, G. (2010). Initiating Curriculum Revision: Exploring the Practices of Educational Developers. *The International Journal for Academic Development*, 15(1), 61–71.

O'Neill, G. (2015). *Curriculum Design in Higher Education: Theory to Practice*. Dublin: UCD Teaching & Learning. www.ucd.ie/t4cms/UCDTLP0068.pdf (accessed 28 September 2022).

Ornstein, A.C., & Hunkins, F.P. (2004). *Curriculum Foundations, Principles and Issues* (3rd ed.). Boston: Allyn and Bacon.

Ornstein, A.C., & Hunkins, F.P. (2009). *Curriculum Foundations, Principles and Issues* (5th ed.). Boston: Allyn and Bacon.

Popham, W.J., & Baker, E.L. (1970). *Establishing Instructional Goals*. Englewood Cliffs, NJ: Prentice-Hall.

Rowntree, D. (1974). *Educational Technology; Curriculum Planning*. London & New York: Harper & Row.

Sadler, D.R. (2010). Beyond Feedback: Developing Student Capability in Complex Appraisal. *Assessment & Evaluation in Higher Education*, 35(5), 535–550.

Schubert, W.H. (1986). *Curriculum: Perspective, Paradigm and Possibility*. New York: Macmillan Publishing Company.

Schweitzer, K. (2020). *Curriculum Design: Definition, Purpose and Types*. www.thoughtco.com/curriculum-design-definition-4154176 (accessed 28 September 2022).

Scriven, M. (1967). The Methodology of Evaluation. In R.E. Stake (Ed.), *Curriculum Evaluation*. Chicago: Rand McNally, American Educational Research Association, pp. 39–83.

Shabatura, J. (2013). *Using Bloom's Taxonomy to Write Effective Learning Objectives*. https://tips.uark.edu/using-blooms-taxonomy/ (accessed 29 September 2022).

Smith, M.K. (1996, 2000). Curriculum Theory and Practice. *The Encyclopaedia of Informal Education*. www.infed.org/biblio/.htm (accessed 28 September 2022).

Stark, J.S. (2000). Planning Introductory College Courses: Content, Context and Form. *Instructional Science*, 28, 413–438.

Stenhouse, L. (1975). *An Introduction to Curriculum Research and Development*. London: Heineman.

Tanner, D., & Tanner, L. (1975). *Curriculum Development: Theory into Practice*. New York: Macmillan.

Toohey, S. (2000). *Beliefs, values and ideologies in course design. In Designing courses for higher education*. (pp. 44–69).

Tyler, R.W. (1949). *Basic Principles of Curriculum and Instruction*. Chicago: University of Chicago Press.

UK The Quality Assurance Agency for Higher Education (2007). *Integrative Assessment: Managing Assessment Practices and Procedure*. www.enhancementthemes.ac.uk/docs/publications/managing-assessment-practices-and-procedures.pdf (accessed 29 September 2022).

Wiggins, G., & McTighe, J. (2010). *Understanding by Design: A Brief Introduction*. Center for Technology & School Change at Teachers College, Columbia University. www.govwentworth.k12.nh.us/schoolfolders/krhs/Understanding%20by%20Design_files/frame.htm (accessed 28 September 2022).

5 Readiness for knowledge integration of Islāmic ethics and Islāmic psychology
An integrated research study

Introduction and context

This chapter is based on a research study undertaken to evaluate the Islāmic moral values of university's lecturers and their perception and attitude towards knowledge integration. This is an abridged version of the research study (Rassool, 2022a). For knowledge integration of Islāmic psychology and Islāmic ethical values in the psychology curriculum to be successful, factors determining the readiness to integrate, both on individual and institutional levels, need to be established and managed effectively before the implementation process commences – that is, integrating Islāmic ethics, studies and worldview with classical and contemporary empirical knowledge of psychology. Despite the "Islāmisation of knowledge" movement and the evolution and development of Islāmic psychology as a discipline, there has been limited integration of knowledge of Islāmic traditions and perspectives in the psychology curriculum in the different educational institutions around the globe.

The Riphah Institute of Clinical and Professional Psychology, Riphah International University, Pakistan, created the Centre for Islāmic Psychology in July 2019. The university was established with an aim to produce professionals with Islāmic moral and ethical values. The Centre for Islāmic Psychology is an initiative to advance the development of a global centre of excellence whose mission is to create and promote the integration of Islāmic ethics and Islāmic psychology in the psychology curriculum. As part of the project on knowledge integration, a thematic analysis of the contents of the psychology curriculum at undergraduate and postgraduate levels were undertaken to assess the contents of the programmes. In the BS in applied psychology programme, there were Islāmic studies with bolt-on module on the teaching of the Qur'ān (life and living). No contents of Islāmic ethics and sciences were identified in the core curriculum of the undergraduate and postgraduate programmes. The Centre for Islāmic Psychology undertook the responsibility to re-evaluate the undergraduate and postgraduate programmes and develop a strategy to integrate Islāmic ethics and Islāmic psychology in those programmes adhering to the core values of Riphah International University.

DOI: 10.4324/9781003329596-5

However, despite the implementation of a series of consultations, workshops, seminars and webinars on curriculum development and restructuring approaches to teaching and learning in Islāmic psychology, there appears to have been a slow process in the implementation of knowledge integration in the curriculum and teaching practices. The urgency to conduct this study was identified when it was observed that in most cases, there has been a lack of readiness and reluctance to integrate knowledge of Islāmic ethical values and Islāmic psychology, hence the rationale for this study.

Literature review

A number of constructs need to be examined in this review in order to provide the scope and context of the study. The constructs include knowledge integration, perception, attitudes, values, role legitimacy, role adequacy and role support. Role legitimacy, role adequacy and role support have been ascribed the label of role behaviours. Since the late 20th century, knowledge integration and integrated research has been used in contemporary Islāmic philosophy to reconcile Islām and modernity and to integrate Islāmic ethics and epistemological values in social sciences. Knowledge integration refers to "the process of merging two or more originally unrelated knowledge structures into a single structure" (Schneider, 2012). However, from an Islāmic perspective, knowledge integration, according to Kasule (2015), "involves integrating Islāmic moral and epistemological values in the various disciplines of knowledge that are taught" (p. 124). Thus, the essence of integrating knowledge, from an Islāmic perspective, is to bring knowledge from the different compartments and sources under one umbrella to achieve a given goal or a set of objectives. Knowledge integration focuses on the integration of empirical evidence (*Ilm 'aqli*) with revealed knowledge (*Ilm 'naqli*) and the synthesis of both sources of knowledge into an integrated model based on Tawhîdic paradigm. This means that knowledge integration is based on reconstructing the epistemology, in the context of psychology, based on the Islāmic worldview. Before examining the literature on knowledge integration in psychology, it is valuable to examine the different approaches of knowledge integration or no integration in Islāmic psychology.

A preliminary investigation on the curriculum development approach and contents analysis of Islāmic psychology and counselling programmes for psychologists in the UK, the USA, and Turkey was undertaken by Rassool (2020). By "hacking" (hacking is a type of research methodology and is a time-honoured Islāmic legal tradition), a number of educational programmes published, on websites on Islāmic psychology and psychotherapy, inferences made to their approaches and contents. Rassool (2020) highlights at least three approaches in curriculum development: the sprinkle approach, the bolt-on approach and the integrated or embedded approach. Recently, a new approach was also included in this model ascribed with the label of globalised approach. Figure 4.1 presents the knowledge integration approach in Islāmic psychology. In this model, four pie-slice-shaped segments can be distinguished, which are interpreted as four distinct approaches in the integration or non-integration of Islāmic psychology and Islāmic ethical values in the psychology curriculum.

Figure 5.1 depicts the models of knowledge integration in Islāmic psychology. The sprinkle approach is based on the principle of randomising Islāmic contents within the curriculum. A few verses of the Qur'ān and Hadīth are interposed at a random basis throughout the educational programme. There is no knowledge integration of Islāmic psychology and Islāmic ethical values in the curriculum contents. The bolt-on approach is where knowledge about Islāmic psychology and ethics are developed independently of the core discipline and, generally, added at the end of the course programme or module. Another variation of this approach is to teach Islāmic psychology and sciences in parallel with secular modern psychology. In this context, there is a lack of integration and Islāmic psychology and sciences are not embedded in the educational programmes.

A third approach identified is the embedded or integrated approach to curriculum development. This approach seeks to break down the barriers of the

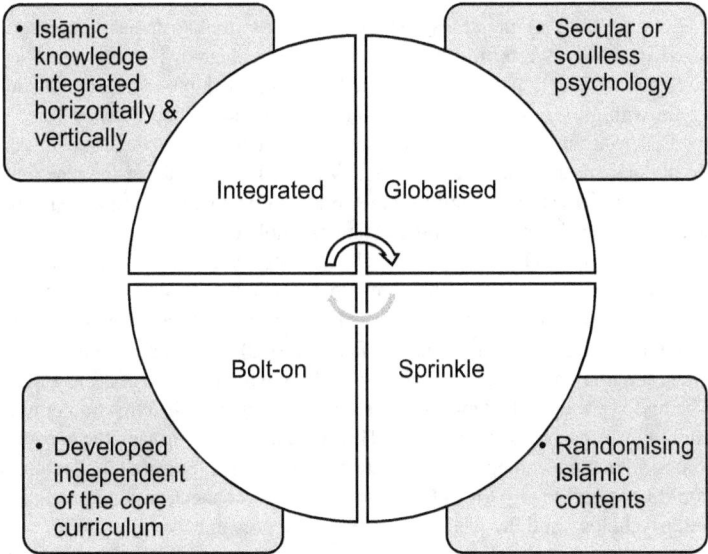

Figure 5.1 Model of knowledge integration
Source: Adapted from Rassool (2020)

traditional curriculum in psychology based on segmentation and isolation of Islāmic ethics and psychology from an Islāmic perspective. This approach is one where subjects are taught through a range of themes, disciplines, and various mechanisms of delivery, as opposed to studying subjects in isolation, like the sprinkle and bolt-on approaches. In the integration of Islāmic knowledge in psychology, Rassool's vertical and horizontal integration model (Rassool, 2020) have been applied. Horizontal integration refers to the relations among various contents, topics and themes involving all domains of knowledge (evidenced-based knowledge, the classical and contemporary work of Islāmic scholars and knowledge based on the Qur'ān and Hadīth. In vertical integration, the educational contents tend to be organised with regard to the sequence and continuity of learning and teaching processes. The most common approach in teaching psychology across most Islāmic academic institutions is the globalised approach. In relation to the effects of globalisation on psychology, this is reflected in this statement:

> Psychological globalisation embraces every country throughout the world and is crystalised as "The Three Worlds of Psychology" In this theory, the United States is considered the first world because to date it is the major producer of psychological knowledge that is exported to the rest of the world.

Rassool (2021a) maintains, "Many Muslim psychologists have been educated in mostly Western universities, or even in their own countries. They have remained in a 'psycho-secular bubble' and turned into clones of Muslim Freud with all the psychobabble and followed blindly their 'Master Voice'" (p. 3). The acceptable face of colonisation of psychology has been substituted by the globalisation of psychology knowledge. This globalised-led teaching, based on the Western-scientific framework, can be characterised as teaching with an emphasis on the Judeo-Christian psychology.

There is limited literature on knowledge integration of Islāmic psychology and Islāmic ethical values in the psychology curriculum. To date, there is only one study that focuses on the implementation of integration on knowledge of Islām and psychology. In a study by Fahmi (2018) on the implementation of integration on knowledge of Islām-psychology with a sample of 32 lecturers. The findings suggest that most of the lecturers thought the Islāmisation of psychology was particularly important. However, most of them lack the capacity to understand psychology from an Islāmic perspective. Some of the lecturers could not provide any logical explanation of the connection between Islām and psychology and the Islāmic perspective on human behaviours. What was interesting with the findings of this study is that none of the psychology lecturers have a background in Islāmic studies. The findings also showed that there was no connection between the integration on psychology and Islām and the developmental of student's knowledge on Islāmic psychology perspective.

The lecturers teach the Islāmic traditions as part of the creed of Islām rather than as an embedded dimension in the psychology curriculum. In a paper on the integration of psychology and theology, Haque (2018) examines the notion of whether

> psychology taught in the Muslim world is compatible with the Islāmic worldview. This question should be asked about all disciplines in humanities and social sciences because they are the ones that shape our intellectual thought process and management of the society.

He went on to discuss how social sciences reflect Western values, concepts and beliefs and secular worldview, which drove all aspects of behaviour, activity and social institutions. Haque (2018) suggests that in order to bring back Muslims' lost intellectual identity, values, legacy and heritage into their curriculum, there is a need to bring Islāmic theology into the equation. He states,

> If we were to integrate psychology and theology, we would examine how modern psychological theories, psychotherapies and research fit in with the Islāmic worldview. We would examine if the present-day theories and practices in psychology are compatible with Islām and an integrated study of psychology and theology.

For course integration, Haque provides a list of themes that can be included in the psychology curriculum rather than the methodology of how to integrate theology in the psychology curriculum. The themes include historical developments from the time when soul was a subject matter of psychology, Islāmic worldviews, Islāmic psychology, Islāmic metaphysics, Islāmic ethics, dimensions of *Fitrah*, the concept of man in Islām (*Ruh, Nafs, Qalb* and their interactions) and contemplation as a form of worship and therapy. In summary, integration of knowledge, from an Islāmic perspective, is the synthesis of divine revelation and acquired knowledge based on the Tawhîdic paradigm. According to this perspective, the process of curriculum organisation represents an effort to enhance the scope, integration, sequence and continuity of knowledge based on Islāmic theological values and practices. There is no contradiction in using both the divine and acquired knowledge as they both are from the same sources. So the problem of duality in Islāmic psychology is resolved.

One of the constructs of this study is perception. There is a relationship between perception and worldview, and the latter is regarded as a personal perception of their relationship with the world. According to Lavrakas (2008),

> Survey questions that assess perception, as opposed to those assessing factual knowledge, are aimed at identifying the processes that (a) underlie how individuals acquire, interpret, organise, and, generally make sense of (i.e. form beliefs about) the environment in which they live; and (b) help measure the extent to which such perceptions affect individual behaviours

and attitudes as a function of an individual's past experiences, biological makeup, expectations, goals, and/or culture.

Perception questions differ from other types of attitudinal questions as the former is how you view the work from an individual lens. In contrast, an attitudinal question is the reaction of an individual's perception of their relationship with the world. The construct of attitude also forms part of the study. That is, an attitude is the way we think (cognitive) and feel (affective) and is reflected in an individual behaviour. According to Glasman and Albarracín (2006), the most powerful influencers of attitude are its importance, its connection with the behaviour, its accessibility, the presence of social pressures, and personal direct experience with the attitude. As previously stated, attitudes have long been known to be predictors of behaviour. Both the theory of planned behaviour and Roger's diffusion of innovation place emphasis on the importance of perception, knowledge and attitudes in the implementation of any new or different practice (Ajzen, 1991; Holt et al., 2010).

Due to limited literature on the factors influencing the integration of Islāmic psychology and ethical values in the psychology curriculum in higher education, there is a need to draw conclusions from other literature and research evidence. For example, several factors influencing technology integration into the learning and teaching process in higher education have been identified. Schiler (2003) identifies a number of variables that can have a significant influence on the adoption of a technology. These include educational level, age, gender, educational experience, experience with computers and attitude towards computers. There is also evidence to suggest that successful implementation of technology integration, attitudes and teacher-related variables are the most powerful predictors of integration (Avidov-Ungar & Eshet-Alkakay, 2011; Becker, 2000). However, if teachers' perceptions are negative, they would result in lack of integration of technology (Hutchison & Reinking, 2011).

In a study by Shaw et al. (1978), the anxieties about role legitimacy, role adequacy and role support have been identified as the contributors to the poor responses by non-specialists in addiction in working with alcohol users. Those workers lacked the authority to intervene because they were uncertain about their professional boundaries. The anxieties about role adequacy are related to the lack of required knowledge, and the lack of role support produced disengagement and inhibited the workers' reluctance to work with alcohol users. Shaw et al. (1978) suggest that the three components are interrelated and that the presence of these factors enhances professional self-esteem, motivation and role fulfilment in working with problem drinkers. In the context of this study, the readiness for knowledge integration by university lecturers may be influenced by role adequacy, role legitimacy and support mechanisms.

The constructs of perception, values and attitudes have long been known to be predictors of behaviour (Ajzen, 1991; Glasman & Albarracín, 2006). In addition, the constructs of role adequacy, role legitimacy and role support have been used previously to explain why various helping professionals are reluctant to take on new dimensions to their professional role (Shaw et al., 1978; Loughran et al., 2010). In the context of this study, role adequacy is defined as having the appropriate knowledge and ethical values to implement knowledge integration, and role legitimacy is the extent to which one has the right to address knowledge integration in psychology. Role support is the provision of professional and personal support at individual and organisational levels. Thus, the aim of this study is to examine the perceptions, values and attitudes of university lecturers on their readiness for knowledge integration of Islāmic psychology and ethical values in the psychology curriculum. In particular, the current research aims to examine the Islāmic moral values of university's lecturers, the perception of knowledge integration and attitude towards knowledge integration. In addition, while this research is exploratory, the following are hypothesised: (1) There will be a significant relationship between Islāmic moral values and the demographic variables. (2) There will be a significant relationship between Islāmic moral values, perception of knowledge integration and attitude towards knowledge integration. (3) Perception of knowledge integration will be better predictors of attitude towards knowledge integration of Islāmic ethics and Islāmic psychology.

Methodology

Sample

This is a convenience or purposive sample of faculty members from each of the four campuses of the Departments of Psychology in a single university in the province of Punjab, Pakistan. The inclusion criteria were that participants must be working currently in one of the four campuses as academic psychologists and/or clinical psychologists.

Design and instrument

This is an integrated research design involving both a quantitative and qualitative research methodologies. Data on the sample were obtained by self-reported questionnaire, which consisted of four sections: Section A is the demographic data (age, gender, position, academic and professional qualification, duration of teaching experiences). Section B consists of an adaptation of the Sahin Index of Islāmic Moral Values (SIIMV) (Francis et al., 2008) which comprises of 17 items. It was constructed around the key Muslim ethical concept *Akhlāq*, meaning disposition, an individual's fundamental value orientation in life and his/her essential nature of being in the world (Francis et al., 2008). Each item is assessed on a close-ended Likert scale ranging from 1 (strongly disagree) to 5 (strongly agree). The SIIMV contains both negative (three) and positive (fourteen) items. The negative items were reverse-scored. The original SIIMV has an alpha coefficient of 0.80, which showed that items are consistent and reliable. The adapted SIIMV has an alpha coefficient of 0.77 (see Table 5.1)

Table 5.1 Reliability of scales, mean, standard deviation and skewness (N = 41)

Assessment Measures	K	X⁻	SD	α	Skewness
Islāmic moral values	17	71.12	7.03	.77	−1.33
Perception of knowledge integration	12	44.56	8.52	.90	−.81
Reflection	5	18.12	3.64	.81	−.77
Participation	3	10.21	3.18	.82	−.41
Motivation	4	16.21	3.04	.78	−1.63
Attitude towards knowledge integration	114.31	30.88	10.55	.93	−.04
Attitude (beliefs, knowledge and confidence; items 1–19)	19	51.29	13.84	.84	.04
Role behaviours (items 20–38)	19	63.02	20.41	.93	.11

K = items, X⁻ = mean, SD = standard deviation, α = Cronbach's alpha

Section C is a questionnaire to examine the lectures' perceptions of knowledge integration. It is an adaption of the Student Perception of Research Integration Questionnaire (SPRIQ) (Visser-Wijnveen et al., 2016), which consists of a 12-item instrument based on three subscales of reflection, participation and motivation. This questionnaire was adapted to form the Lecturer's Perceptions of Knowledge Integration Questionnaire (LPKIQ-12). The LPKIQ-12 consists of three constructs of participation (three items), motivation (four items) and reflection (five items). The construct of participation includes items on the involvement of lecturers in knowledge integration and their contributions. The construct of reflection includes items focusing on attention being paid to the knowledge integration process leading to implementation. The construct of motivation consists of items concerning an increase in lecturers' enthusiasm and interest for knowledge integration. The items were scored on a five-point Likert scale, ranging from "very rarely" to "very frequently." The adapted LPKIQ-12 has an alpha coefficient of 0.90.

Section D consists of a questionnaire measuring the attitudes of university lecturers towards integrating and teaching Islāmic psychology and Islāmic ethical values in the psychology curriculum. The Attitude Questionnaire Towards Knowledge Integration (AQTKI) is a 38-item measure that identifies beliefs, knowledge and confidence (items 1–19). Items 20–38 are an adaptation from the subscales of role adequacy, role legitimacy and role support of the Adolescent Substance Use Problems Perceptions Questionnaire (ASUPPQ) (Connors et al., 2019).The adaptations were made by substantially changing the wording to reflect the scope of the study, and in some cases, new statements were included. There are seven possible responses to each item on a scale of "strongly agree" to "strongly disagree." Low scores denote positive attitudes, whereas high scores are associated with negative views. Several of the items are worded negatively. These are items 2, 10, 12, 16 and 17. The scores for these items would be reversed before tallying a total score for the entire questionnaire. The minimum possible score is 38 and the maximum is 154. The adapted AQTKI has an alpha coefficient of 0.93.

Data collection and analysis

Data collection was completed in June and July 2022. Data analyses were performed using version 22 of the Statistical Package for the Social Sciences (IBM PASW Statistics 22). In addition, descriptive statistics were used to evaluate and analyse the data for the means and standard deviations. Demographic variables were analysed by using frequency distributions and percentages. For inferential statistics, the study employed Pearson's correlation, reliability and multiple linear regressions for data analyses. For the qualitative analysis, the focus interviews were audio-recorded and transcribed verbatim with anonymisation, and the audio recordings were deleted following transcription. By using thematic analysis, meaningful themes from the data were identified. The framework for thematic analysis was used – compiling, disassembling, assembling, interpreting and concluding – and guided by a set of questions (Castleberry & Nolen, 2018). Six participants were recruited for the focus interviews.

Ethical considerations

Ethical approval of the study was approved by the Riphah Institute of Clinical and Professional Psychology Research and Ethics Committee. General information and a consent form were provided to participants taking part in the study. All participants were provided with information regarding their role in the study, the purpose of the study and the data collection methods. Participants were informed that they have the right to withdraw from the study at any time during any of the procedures. All of the lecturers' interviews and the results of questionnaires adhered to the proviso of confidentiality and anonymity.

Findings

A total of 41 university lecturers completed the study with the majority being of females (85.4%). The majority of the sample belonged to the 21–34-year age group (68.3%). The most frequently reported postgraduate qualifications were master's degrees (68.3%), followed by PhDs (31.7%). The teaching experiences of the sample were as follows: with less than five years of teaching experience (46.3%), between five to ten years of teaching experience (39.1%) and over ten years of teaching experience (12.2%). The demographic profiles of the participants are reported in Table 5.2.

Sahin Index of Islāmic Moral Values

Table 5.3 displays the frequency and percentage (high and low values) and mean and standard deviation of the level of Islāmic moral values of lecturers (N = 41) based on the Shin Index of Islāmic Moral Values. The mean level of

Table 5.2 Demographic profile of the sample (N = 41)

Demographic characteristics		f	%
Age	20–34 years	28	68.3
	35–54 years	11	26.8
	55–60 years	2	4.9
Gender	Male	6	14.6
	Female	35	85.4
Education	Master's degree	28	68.3
	PhD	13	31.7
Teaching experience	Less than 5 years	19	46.3
	5–10 years	16	39.1
	11–20 years	4	9.8
	21–40 years	1	2.4
	More than 40 years	1	2.4
Institutional setting	Lahore	13	31.7
	Islamabad	17	41.5
	Faisalabad	11	26.8

Note: f = frequency, % = percentage

Table 5.3 Frequency and percentage (high and low values), mean and standard deviation of the level of Islāmic moral values of lecturers (N = 41)

Assessment measures	f (%) High value	f (%) Low value	$\bar{X}$	SD
I believe honesty is always good regardless of the consequences.	41 (100)	0 (0.0)	4.68	.47
I try hard to be a good role model for my students.	36 (87.8)	5 (12.2)	4.12	.95
I do not hide my mistake if I knew it would hurt me.	35 (85.4)	6 (14.6)	4.02	.88
I feel bad when someone damages another's properties.	40 (97.6)	1 (2.4)	4.61	.73
I do not think that I am a good role model for others.*	25 (61.0)	16 (39.0)	3.49	1.09
I admire friends who listen to their seniors' advice.	37 (90.2)	4 (9.8)	4.22	.69
I do not attempt to lie when I face a critical situation.	31 (75.6)	10 (24.4)	3.88	.84
I feel happy when others are satisfied with my behaviour.	39 (95.1)	2 (4.9)	4.49	.59
I do not like to follow the advice given by my seniors.*	34 (82.9)	7 (17.1)	4.17	.89
I hate watching movies with low or negative moral values.	31 (75.6)	10 (24.4)	4.02	1.03
I avoid friendships with people who smoke.	25 (61.0)	16 (39.0)	3.66	1.15
I have not attempted to cheat ever in my life.	33 (80.5)	8 (19.5)	4.00	1.14
I hate to listen to my seniors' advice.*	38 (92.7)	3 (7.3)	4.44	.77
I like to participate as a volunteer.	31 (75.6)	10 (24.4)	4.10	1.06
My freedom should not conflict with anothers' freedom.	32 (78.0)	9 (22.0)	4.07	.84
I feel pain when moral crimes increase in society.	38 (92.7)	3 (7.3)	4.54	.95
I encourage equal opportunities among people.	38 (92.7)	3 (7.3)	4.61	.77
Total score	34 (82.93)	7 (17.07)	71.12	7.03

Note: f = frequency, % = percentage, $\bar{X}$ = mean, SD = standard deviation

Islāmic moral values of lecturers is 71.12 ($X^- = 4.18$) and the standard deviation is 7.03. Most of the items have high values on mean average values ranging from 3.49 to 4.68 (maximum 5). The findings showed that 34 lecturers (83%) obtained high value score, which indicated high Islāmic moral values and 7 lecturers (17%) obtained low score on the scale.

Perceptions of knowledge integration and attitude towards knowledge integration

Table 5.4 depicts the findings of the questionnaires of perceptions of knowledge integration and attitude towards knowledge integration. The findings from the Perception of Knowledge Integration Questionnaire revealed overall the higher percentage of low scores (58.54%). In addition, both the subscales of reflection (60.98%) and participation (60.98%) showed lower scores, thus indicating a low level of reflection and participation towards knowledge integration. However, the high scores the motivation subscale (68.29%) indicated that the lecturers were much more motivated to learn about knowledge integration. The Attitude Towards Knowledge Integration questionnaire showed that a low overall score (87.80%). The subscales of attitude (beliefs, knowledge and confidence, items 1–19) showed a high percentage of low scores (97.56%), which indicated a significantly positive attitude towards knowledge integration of Islāmic ethics and Islāmic psychology.

Role behaviours (role legitimacy, role adequacy and role support)

The findings of the third subscale of the attitude towards knowledge integration revealed a high percentage of low scores (68.29%) in role behaviour (role adequacy, role legitimacy and role support). The high percentage of low scores was also identified in additional subscales: role adequacy (58.50%), role legitimacy (78.00%) and role support (75.60%).

Table 5.4 Perceptions of knowledge integration *and* attitude towards knowledge integration

Scales	I	f/% High score	f/% Low score
Perceptions of knowledge integration	12	17 (41.46)	24 (58.54)
Reflection	5	16 (39.02)	25 (60.98)
Participation	3	16 (39.02)	25 (60.98)
Motivation	4	28 (68.29)	13 (31.71)
Attitude towards knowledge integration	38	5 (12.20)	36 (87.80)
Attitude beliefs, knowledge and confidence (items 1–19)	19	1 (2.44)	40 (97.56)

Note: I = number of items, f = frequency, % = percentage

Association between study variables

A one-way ANOVA was performed to compare the effect of Islāmic moral values on the sample demographic variables. Two demographic variables were identified as having statistically significant relationships. The demographic variables of age (F = 2.179, p = 045) and length of teaching experiences (F = 2.596, p = .019) (see Table 5.6).

Table 5.7 presents the correlation between Islāmic moral values, perception of knowledge integration and attitude towards knowledge integration. The perception of knowledge integration was negatively correlated with attitude towards knowledge integration ($\gamma = 31$, $p < .05$). In the perception of knowledge integration subscales, reflection was negatively correlated with

Table 5.5 Study variables of role behaviours

Scales	*I*	*f (%)* High score	*f (%)* Low score
Role behaviours	19	13 (31.71)	28 (68.29)
Role adequacy	8	17 (41.50)	24 (58.50)
Role legitimacy	5	9 (22.00)	32 (78.00)
Role support	6	10 (24.40)	31 (75.60)

Note: *I* = items, *f* = frequency, % = percentage

Table 5.6 ANOVA: summary of selected variables

	Sum of squares	df	Mean square	F	Sig.
Age	9.262	20	.463	2.179	.045
Years of teaching experiences	24.228	20	1.211	2.596	.019

Table 5.7 Correlation between Islāmic moral values, perception of knowledge integration and attitude towards knowledge integration in university lecturers (N = 41)

Scales	1	2	3	4	5	6	7	8	M	SD
1 Islāmic moral values	-	.04	.90	-.07	.08	-.19	-.20	-.16	71.12	7.03
2 Perception of knowledge integration		-	.92**	.83**	.82**	-.31*	-.26	-.29	44.56	8.52
3 Reflection (subscale)			-	.67**	.67**	-.41**	-.34*	-.38*	18.12	3.64
4 Participation (subscale)				-	.48**	-.25	-.22	-.22	10.21	3.18
5 Motivation (subscale)					-	-.19	-.07	-.12	16.21	3.04
6 Attitude towards knowledge integration						-	.85**	.93**	30.88	10.55
7 Belief, knowledge and confidence (subscale)							-	.61**	51.29	13.84
8 Role behaviours (role legitimacy, role adequacy and role support) (subscale)								-	63.02	20.41

Note: **Correlation is significant at the 0.01 level (two-tailed). *Correlation is significant at the 0.05 level (two-tailed).

Readiness for knowledge integration of Islām 73

attitude towards knowledge integration ($\gamma = -.41$, p < .01), negatively correlated with attitude (belief, knowledge, and confidence ($\gamma = -.34$, p < .05) and significantly negatively associated with role behaviours (role legitimacy, role adequacy and role support) ($\gamma = -.38$, p < .05).

One of the hypotheses tested is that the perception of knowledge integration (subscales of reflection, participation and motivation) will be a predictor of attitude towards knowledge integration (subscales of belief, knowledge and confidence). Tables 5.8 to 5.10 present the findings of the regression analysis. The findings showed that the perception of knowledge integration subscale reflection is a significant predictor of attitude towards knowledge integration (***$p < .001$) (Table 5.8), a predictor of the subscale attitude (***p < .001) (Table 5.9) and a predictor of attitude subscale role behaviours (role legitimacy, role adequacy and role support) (***$p < .001$) (Table 5.10).

Table 5.8 Regression coefficients of Islāmic moral values, perception of knowledge integration and attitude towards knowledge integration

Variable	B	β	SE
Constant	177.85***		22.84
Reflection	−3.50	−.41	
R^2	0.17		
ΔR^2	0.15		

Note: ***$p < .001$, β = standardised coefficient, SE = standard error, R^2 = R square, ΔR^2 = Adjusted R square

Table 5.9 Regression coefficients of Islāmic moral values, perception of knowledge integration and attitude towards knowledge integration

Variable	B	β	SE
Constant	75.36***		10.53
Reflection	−1.32	−.34	
R^2	0.12		
ΔR^2	0.10		

Note: ***$p < .001$, β = standardised coefficient, SE = standard error, R^2 = R square, ΔR^2 = Adjusted R square

Table 5.10 Regression coefficients of Islāmic moral values, perception of knowledge integration and attitude towards knowledge integration

Variable	B	β	SE
Constant	102.49***		15.28
Reflection	−2.17	−.38	
R^2	0.15		
ΔR^2	0.12		

Note. ***$p < .001$, β = standardised coefficient, SE = standard error, R^2 = R square, ΔR^2 = Adjusted R square

Qualitative data: thematic analysis

Though this study was intended to focus on the perception of and attitude towards knowledge integration of Islāmic ethics and psychology in teaching practices, the focus interviews allowed for the emergence of themes supplementary to the initial research focus. The focus interview questions were phrased such that lecturers were asked whether they address Islāmic ethics or Islāmic psychology in their teaching practice and to identify the barriers in preventing knowledge integration and facilitators that may be supportive in knowledge integration. After thematic analysis, six themes were identified.

Theme 1: Barriers in preventing knowledge integration

Most participants described the lack of preparation, lack of knowledge, lack of experts and lack of resources (books, materials) and having no guidance as the main barriers in the prevention of knowledge integration in teaching practices.

> *I have no idea regarding Islāmic psychology. I learned about Muslim psychology, which is different from Islāmic psychology. There is a lack of preparation, lack of experts. In Pakistan, they discourage Islāmic psychology. It is not part of modern psychology. Lack of knowledge and training. Islāmic psychology is a sensitive issue and we will not apply anything without knowledge or training. Not having Islāmic tools, lack of resources. We don't have field experts with reference to knowledge integration of Islāmic psychology and Islāmic ethical values in the psychology curriculum. So, initially the lack of guidance and proper practice was the main concerns. Lack of resources and adequate time are the main reasons. Official schedule and timetable by the department. Means time issue as primary concern. Secondly, enough reading material and resources are not there in the library and it is very expensive if I want to purchase it. Lack of expert advice in curriculum planning. No support from anyone.*

Theme 2: Facilitators in enhancing knowledge integration

Most participants suggested that having facilitators, workshops and courses in Islāmic psychology and psychotherapy has helped them with their teaching practices. One participant mentioned that having taught both Islāmic studies and psychology has helped with knowledge integration.

> *The course (5 day course on Foundation of Islāmic Psychology & Psychotherapy). Training. Having taught Islāmic studies and psychology. Those who have basic knowledge regarding curriculum development with reference to Islāmic psychology and Islāmic ethical values. Colleagues and available resources in the department and library.*

Theme 3: Role in knowledge integration

In relation to the legitimacy of the role of the participants in knowledge integration, most of the interviewees reported that this is part of their role. The lecturers have a strong conviction that it is their professional responsibility as Muslim psychologists to address knowledge integration.

It is our role... As a Muslim, I have a main role as clinical psychologist to introduce the students with... Allah. It is my role as a Muslim. It is our duty to teach IP [Islāmic psychology] to inculcate Islāmic concepts in psychology. It is our responsibility. Psychology is related to Islām. Yes, as I am a lecturer and a practicing psychologist.

Theme 4: Addressing Islāmic ethics or Islāmic psychology in teaching/clinical practice

There were mixed responses regarding knowledge integration of Islāmic ethics and Islāmic psychology in teaching practice. The majority of the participants did not address Islāmic ethics or Islāmic psychology in teaching or clinical practice. Just a few were involved in this process, as stated in the following statements.

Yes, in my mentoring session mostly, students face a lot of problems when it comes to religion. I address Islāmic ethics and psychology in my teaching due to studying Muslim psychology in my master's degree. I teach professional ethics and I relate Islāmic ethics in my teaching. Yes, Alhamdulliah, now I can address Islāmic ethics or Islāmic psychology in my teachings. I had inculcated Islāmic ethics/practices in few subjects of undergraduate and postgraduate studies in psychology.

Theme 5: Readiness for knowledge integration

All the participants reported that they were ready for knowledge integration. This suggests they are highly motivated.

Most said yes. Deep connection with my Allah. I have experience in Islāmic psychology. Yes, I am ready for knowledge integration of Islāmic psychology and Islāmic ethical values in the psychology curriculum.

Theme 6: Training needs

Most participants reported the need for the adequate preparation for knowledge integration. The following statements echoed these sentiments.

More courses and updating the curriculum. Study circles would play an important role in the preparation. Short workshops. Motivation and resource materials. More knowledge on Islāmic sciences. More resources are needed. More training more practical sessions. Proper literature and curriculum development guidelines. Courses on clinical application of Islāmic psychotherapy. Training in knowledge integration and knowledge about Islām and then Islāmic psychology.

Discussion

The purpose of this study was to examine the Islāmic moral values of university lecturers and their perception of and attitude towards knowledge integration. The study also tested some hypotheses to determine the relationship between Islāmic moral values and the demographic variables and perception of and attitude towards knowledge integration of Islāmic ethics and Islāmic psychology. The qualitative findings enhance the findings of the current quantitative study by providing insight into the experiences of the participants. Given the importance of knowledge integration of Islāmic ethics and Islāmic psychology in the psychology curriculum at university level (Rassool, 2020), this exploratory study may be viewed as an agenda-setting for further research. With the majority of the sample having high Islāmic moral values (83%), religious and ethical values (*Akhlāq*) seem to play an important role in the lives of the majority of the lecturers. The high level of Islāmic moral values can be interpreted in at least two ways. A first explanation focuses on the demographic profile of the sample. The lecturers, being all Muslims, must have contained highly devout individuals adhering to the morals of the Islāmic jurisprudence (*Shari'ah*). There is evidence to suggest that "Muslims widely hold the view that it is necessary to believe in God to be moral and have good values" (Pew Research Center, 2013). In addition, the university may have attracted individuals who adhere to the Islāmic core values of the university. This expected outcome is in line with the mission and core values of the university. The university values include *Muhasabah* (accountability), *Ijtimaiyyah* (teamwork), *Mushawarah* (consultation and harmony), *Rahmah* (compassion), *Itqan* (pursuit of excellence) and *Al Akhirah* (*Akhirah*-oriented decision).

The participants had an overall the higher percentage of low scores in both the subscales of reflection (60.98%) and participation (60.98%), thus indicating a low level of reflection and participation towards knowledge integration. This is an expected outcomes as the participants lack the necessary knowledge about Islāmic psychology and ethical values, and most of them are not familiar with the methodology of knowledge integration. The lack of reflective practice time for knowledge integration may also have inhibited knowledge integration (MacDonald et al., 2005). In addition, the sample reported making limited contribution to knowledge integration and paid restricted attention to the recent developments in the field. In contrast, the high percentage of low scores on the motivation subscale (68.29%) indicated that the lecturers were highly motivated to learn about Islāmic psychology and knowledge integration. Most of the participants were enthusiastic and motivated to learn more about Islāmic psychology and ethical values, which have enhanced their understanding of the most important concepts in the domain of Islāmic psychology. Their increase in motivation may also be the result of the departments of psychology encouraging the lecturers to integrate Islāmic ethics and Islāmic psychology in their teaching practices. The literature from other fields supports a relationship between motivations and adoption of technology. Motivational factors, including achievement, compensation, personal growth, administrative support and personal fulfilment, are key components in the adoption and use of technology (Betts, 1998; Lawler & King, 2003). The same motivational factors may be at work in the domain of knowledge integration. The findings from the Attitude Towards Knowledge Integration Questionnaire showed that a high percentage of participants (N = 36) with an overall score (87.80%). The subscales of attitude (beliefs, knowledge and confidence (items 1–19) showed a high percentage of low scores (97.56%), which indicated a significantly positive attitude towards knowledge integration of Islāmic ethics and Islāmic psychology. From the literature on the information and communication technology (ICT) in the classroom, there is evidence to suggest that university teachers' perceptions, attitudes, and motivation are significant factors in predicting ICT integration in the classroom (Zamir & Thomas, 2019). The literature also provides ample evidence that attitude is one of the many factors that influence teachers' ICT use (Semerci & Aydin, 2018).

The second component of the Attitude Towards Knowledge Integration Questionnaire is role behaviours, which are a combination of role adequacy, role legitimacy and role support. The high percentage of low scores of the participants on the role behaviours' subscales (68.29%) indicated a significantly positive attitude towards knowledge integration of Islāmic ethics and Islāmic psychology. The constructs of role adequacy and role legitimacy are possible keys to understanding the mechanism behind the adoption of new ideas and intervention (Loughran et al., 2010). The percentage in the total scores of the role adequacy subscale is low (58.50%) as compared to role legitimacy (78.00%) and role support (75.60%). This may indicate that the lecturers experienced a high level of role inadequacy. This means not having the appropriate knowledge and ethical values to implement knowledge integration in their teaching practices. Factors that negatively affect role adequacy include low awareness, lack of knowledge and perceived lack of expertise (Nolan et al., 2012). The findings also showed a high percentage of low scores on the role legitimacy subscale. This is the extent to which one has the right to address knowledge integration in psychology. This current finding is confirmed from the identified themes in the qualitative findings of this study. In relation to the legitimacy of their role, most of the interviewees reported that this is part of their role and that it is their professional responsibility as Muslim psychologists to address knowledge integration. The participants have a clear idea of their obligations to the university to inculcate Islāmic ethical values in their role as lecturers and in integrating Islāmic psychology and ethical values as part of their teaching practices. For role support (75.60%), the participants reported that they could easily find someone who would help them clarify their professional responsibilities and discuss any issues they encounter in knowledge integration. This professional and personal support are both at individual and organisational levels. There is evidence to suggest that the strongest predictors of role legitimacy and role adequacy were support and the perceived usefulness of education (Loughran et al., 2010; Skinner et al., 2009). Education and training play a major role in the development of both role adequacy and legitimacy (Loughran et al., 2010; Skinner et al., 2009).

Qualitative data illustrated some of the ways in which the lecturers' perception and attitude towards may impact on knowledge integration in teaching practices. The participants described the lack of preparation, knowledge, experts, guidance and resources (books, materials) as the main barriers in the prevention of knowledge integration in teaching practices. These barriers may be considered as inhibitors of the role adequacy of the participants. In the literature, the factors that inhibit faculty to implement teaching innovation are workload concerns, negative comments made by colleagues, training, lack of support and minimal release time provided by their department (Schifter, 2000). In addition, organisational-level predictors of implementation success include structure (Zaltman et al., 1973), strategy (Nicholson et al., 1990), financial resources (Mohr, 1969) and organisational culture (Damanpour, 1991). The main facilitators in enhancing knowledge integration that were identified by the participants include having more workshops and courses in Islāmic psychology and psychotherapy. One interesting finding described by a participant is having knowledge in both Islāmic studies and psychology would enable knowledge integration in teaching practices.

The qualitative data also add a new dimension to the quantitative results regarding the issue of role adequacy and legitimacy. There was a wide consensus that it is the legitimate role of the participants to be involved in knowledge integration of Islāmic ethics and Islāmic psychology, being their responsibilities as Muslim psychologists. The issue of role legitimacy is confirmed in both qualitative and quantitative findings of the sample. In addition, the findings showed that the participants were highly motivated. These findings are supported in the literature that show that role legitimacy is the primary predictor of motivation (Skinner et al., 2009). The literature also suggests that the individual characteristics that predict implementation of innovation include personality (Barron & Harrington, 1981), motivation (Axtell et al., 2000), cognitive ability (West, 1987) and job characteristics (Brinkerhoff, 2006). Though all the participants in the study have the readiness for knowledge integration, most of them failed to implement knowledge integration in their teaching practices due to role inadequacy and lack of requisite knowledge in Islāmic ethics and Islāmic psychology. Most participants reported the need for "More resources. More training. More practical sessions," "Proper literature and curriculum development guidelines," and "Training in knowledge integration and knowledge about Islām and then Islāmic psychology." The literature suggests that the efficacy of lecturers are enhanced by professional development (Brinkerhoff, 2006), support from their colleagues (Tilton & Hartnett, 2016), and sufficient knowledge (Abbitt, 2011).

Limitations of the study

This study has some limitations; the findings specifically relate to a particular university in Pakistan, with a limited segment of university lecturers, and the study is not generalisable beyond this university because this is a single case study. The self-selected group of lecturers may be different in personality, interest and motivation in Islāmic psychology as compared to other Muslim psychologists. The selection of participants in the study produced convenience samples to test the hypotheses, and this sampling mode is open to researcher bias, and this affects representativeness. In addition, a convenience sample does not control for threats to internal and external validity. Random (for example, probability) sampling offers the best chance of minimising selection effects because, theoretically, each person in the population has a known chance of being chosen for participation. Even though probability samples can be biased because not all eligible persons agree to participate, these samples should result in significantly less bias than those developed using convenience methods. However, Polit and Hungler (1999) have argued that any sampling method cannot guarantee representativeness unless data from the whole population is collected. Hence, one must assume that the sample possesses some local representation as opposed to a national one.

Another limitation is the use of self-reported questionnaires, and it is possible that participants might not be completely forthcoming with their experiences, and their responses may be subject to social desirability bias. The collection of data for this study was based on a number of self-reported questionnaires based on a variety of formats. This could lead to survey fatigue, which can have adverse effects on quality of response rates. In addition, despite the reliability of all the questionnaires, there is a need to ascertain their validity and subjected to factor analysis to determine the subscales of the instruments. There is also inherent subjectivity in the analysis of qualitative research. However, despite the lack of transferability of the findings and its limitations, it can be seen as indicative of our understanding of how lecturers perceive the integration of knowledge of Islāmic psychology and Islāmic ethical values in the psychology curriculum. Thus, the generalisations of these findings are limited to this particular university and departments of psychology.

Conclusion

This exploratory study aimed to improve our understanding of the way in which university lecturers perceive and experience knowledge integration of Islāmic psychology and Islāmic ethical values in their teaching practices. The first major practical contribution of the present study is that it provides much-needed empirical data on the perceptions, attitudes and role behaviours of university lecturers' readiness for knowledge integration. The findings of the study have implications in the implementation of knowledge integration of Islāmic psychology and Islāmic ethics in both the teaching practices and the psychology curriculum in psychology departments. An important implication of the study will point to a specific set of individual moral values that may enhance the readiness of university lecturers towards knowledge integration The findings of the study have implications at both individual and organisational level.

At the individual level, the findings of the study have implications for educators' teaching-learning and evaluating strategies in enhancing knowledge, skills and attitudes in knowledge integration of Islāmic psychology and Islāmic ethics in psychology curriculum. There is a need to adequately prepare the lectures in Islāmic studies despite their high Islāmic morality values. Another implication stems from the identification of potential barriers and potential facilitators that may support, foster or hamper the implementation knowledge integration at the organisational level. This has implications in the evaluation of the process of knowledge implementation in the curriculum at organisational level. Moreover, the analysis that is presented in this study conveyed valuable information for future research that will explore the various methodologies in knowledge integration. In addition to this, the overview presented in this research will push for new paradigms which will be useful for future discussion and implementation of knowledge integration. However, for proper implementation of knowledge integration in both the psychology curriculum and teaching practices, we need to move beyond just the provision of education and training.

Recommendations for education and policy-makers

- Promote and strengthen the knowledge integration in the psychology curriculum.
- Continue to recruit individuals who adhere to the Islāmic core values of the university.
- Provide more strategic education and training to increase role adequacy and role legitimacy.
- Promote more informal seminars and discussion groups on Islāmic psychology.

- Select core young lecturers to be coached and mentored on Islāmic psychology and Islāmic sciences.
- Provide more support and supervision for lecturers by specialists in Islāmic psychology and psychotherapy.
- Provide more resources in Islāmic psychology and psychotherapy (books, audio-visual aids, journals, etc.) to be made available and accessible to all the lecturers.

Bibliography

Abbitt, J.T. (2011). An Investigation of the Relationship Between Self-Efficacy Beliefs about Technology Integration and Technological Pedagogical Content Knowledge (TPACK) Among Preservice Teachers. *Journal of Digital Learning in Teacher Education*, 27(4), 134–143.

Ajzen, I. (1991). The Theory of Planned Behaviour. *Organizational Behavior and Human Decision Processes*, 50(2), 179–211.

Avidov-Ungar, O., & and Eshet-Alkakay, Y. (2011). Lecturers in a World of Change: Lecturers' Knowledge and Attitudes Towards the Implementation of Innovative Technologies in Schools. *Interdisciplinary Journal of e-Learning and Lifelong Learning*, 7(2011), 291–303.

Axtell, C.M., Holman, D.J., Unsworth, K.L., Wall, T.D., Waterson, E.P., & Harrington, E. (2000). Shopfloor Innovation: Facilitating the Suggestion and Implementation of Ideas. *Journal of Occupational and Organizational Psychology*, 73, 265–285.

Barron, F., & Harrington, D.M. (11981). Creativity, Intelligence, and Personality. *Annual Review of Psychology*, 32, 439–476.

Becker, H.J. (2000). Findings from the Teaching, Learning, and Computing Survey: Is Larry Cuban Right? *Education Policy Analysis Archives*, 8(51). https://doi.org/10.14507/epaa.v8n51.2000.

Betts, K.S. (1998). *Factors Influencing Faculty Participation in Distance Education in Postsecondary Education in the United States: An Institutional Study.* Unpublished doctoral dissertation. Washington, DC: George Washington University.

Brinkerhoff, J. (2006). Effects of a Long-Duration, Professional Development Academy on Technology Skills, Computer Self-Efficacy, and Technology Integration Beliefs and Practices. *Journal of Research on Technology in Education*, 39, 22–43.

Castleberry, A., & Nolen, A. (2018). Thematic Analysis of Qualitative Research Data: Is it as Easy as it Sounds? *Currents in Pharmacy Teaching and Learning*, 10(6), 807–815.

Connors, E., McKenzie, M., Robinson, P., Tager, M., Scardamalia, K., Oros, M., & Hoover, S. (2019). Adaptation of the Drug and Drug Problems Perception Questionnaire to Assess Healthcare Provider Attitudes Toward Adolescent Substance Use. *Preventive Medicine Reports*, 14, 100852. http://doi.org/10.1016/j.pmedr.2019.100852.

Damanpour, F. (1991). Organizational Innovation: A Meta-Analysis of Effects of Determinants and Moderators. *Academy of Management Journal*, 34, 555–590.

Fahmi, R. (2018).The Implementation of Integration on Knowledge: Islām-Psychology Research. *Journal of Politics, Economics and Management*, 6(1), 63–67.

Francis, L.J., Şahin, A., & Failakawi, F. (2008). Sahin Index of Islāmic Moral Values. Psychometric Properties of Two Islāmic Measures among Young Adults in Kuwait:

The Sahin-Francis Scale of Attitude toward Islām and the Sahin Index of Islāmic Moral Values. *Journal of Muslim Mental Health*, 3(1), 9–24.

Glasman, L.R., & Albarracín, D. (2006). Forming Attitudes that Predict Future Behavior: A Meta-Analysis of the Attitude-Behavior Relation. *Psychological Bulletin*, 132(5), 778–822.

Haque, A. (2018). *Integration of Psychology and Theology*. Paper Presented at the Faculty of Theology, Aligarh Muslim University on the 1st of January 2018.

Holt, D.T., Helfrich, C.D., Halland, C., & Weiner, B.J. (2010). Are You Ready? How Health Professionals Can Comprehensively Conceptualize Readiness for Change. *Journal of General Internal Medicine*, 25(1), 50–55.

Hutchison, A., & Reinking, D. (2011). Teachers' Perceptions of Integrating Information and Communication Technologies into Literacy Instruction: A National Survey in the U.S. *Reading Research Quarterly*, 46(4), 308–329.

Kasule, O.H. (2015). Integration of Knowledge (IOK) and Textbook Writing for Islāmic Universities. *International Journal of Islāmic Thoughts*, 4(1), 123–126.

Lavrakas, P.J. (2008). *Encyclopedia of Survey Research Methods* (Vols. 1–0). Thousand Oaks, CA: Sage Publications, Inc.

Lawler, P.A., & King, K.P. (2003). *New Perspectives on Designing and Implementing Professional Development of Teachers of Adults*. Chester, PA: Widener University.

Loughran, H., Hohman, M., & Finnegan, D. (2010).Predictors of Role Legitimacy and Role Adequacy of Social Workers Working with Substance-Using Clients. *The British Journal of Social Work*, 40(1), 239–256.

MacDonald, K., Yanchar, S.C., & Osguthrope, R.T. (2005). Addressing Faculty Concerns about Distance Learning. *Online Journal of Distance Learning Administration*, 8(4), 1–12.

Mohr, L.B. (1969). Determinants of Innovation in Organizations. *American Political Science Review*, 63, 111–126.

Nicholson, N., Rees, A., & Brooks-Rooney, A. (1990). Strategy, Innovation, and Performance. *Journal of Management Studies*, 27, 511–534.

Nolan, C., Deehan, A., Wylie, A., & Jones, R. (2012). Practice Nurses and Obesity: Professional and Practice-Based Factors Affecting Role Adequacy and Role Legitimacy. *Primary Health Care Research & Development*, 13(4), 353–363.

Pew Research Center. (2013). Chapter 3 Morality. www.pewresearch.org/religion/2013/04/30/the-worlds-muslims-religion-politics-society-morality/ (accessed 6 October 2022).

Polit, D.F., & Hungler, B. (1999). *Nursing Research: Principles and Methods 6th Edition*. Philadelphia: J.B. Lippincott.

Rassool, G.H. (2020). Cognitive Restructuring of Psychology: The Case for a Vertical and Horizontal Integrated, Embedded Curriculum Model for Islāmic Psychology. *Islāmic Studies*, 59(4), 477–494.

Rassool, G.H. (2021a). *Islāmic Psychology: Human Behaviour and Experiences from an Islāmic Perspective*. Oxford: Routledge.

Rassool, G.H. (2021b). Decolonising Psychology and Its (Dis) Contents. In G.H. Rassool (Ed.), *Islāmic Psychology: Human Behaviour and Experiences from an Islāmic Perspective*. Oxford: Routledge, pp. 583–601.

Rassool, G.H. (2022a). *Islām and Psychology Nexus: Perception Attitudes and Role Behaviours of University Lecturers on Their Readiness for Knowledge Integration of Islāmic Psychology and Ethical Values in The Psychology Curriculum: A Case*

Study of a Pakistani University. Submitted for the Postgraduate Certificate in Islāmic Thought and Knowledge Integration, IKI Academy by the Institute of Knowledge Integration and the International Institute of Islāmic Thought (IIIT).

Rassool, G.H. (2022b). *Foundation of Islāmic Psychology: From Classical Scholars to Contemporary Thinkers*. Oxford: Routledge.

Schifter, C.C. (2000). Faculty Participation in Asynchronous Learning Networks: A Case Study of Motivating and Inhibiting Factors. *Journal of Asynchronous Learning Networks*, 4(1), 15–22.

Schiler, J. (2003). Working with ICT: Perceptions of Australian Principals. *Journal of Educational Administration*, 41(3), 171–185.

Schneider, M. (2012). Knowledge Integration. In S.S. Seel (Eds.), *Encyclopedia of the Sciences of Learning*. Boston, MA: Springer.

Semerci, A., & Aydin, M.K. (2018). Examining High School Teachers' Attitudes Towards ICT Use in Education. *International Journal of Progressive Education*, 14(2), 93–105.

Shaw, S., Cartwright, A., Spratley, T., & Harwin, J. (1978). *Responding to Drinking Problems*. London: Croom Helm.

Skinner, N., Roche, A., Freeman, T., & Addy, D. (2009). Responding to Alcohol and Other Drug Issues: The Effect of Role Adequacy and Role Legitimacy on Motivation and Satisfaction. *Drugs: Education, Prevention, and Policy*, 12, 449–463.

Tilton, J., & Hartnett, M. (2016). What Are the Influences on Teacher Mobile Technology Self-Efficacy in Secondary School Classrooms? *Journal of Open, Flexible and Distance Learning*, 20(2), 79–93.

Visser-Wijnveen, G.J., van der Rijst, R.M., & van Driel, J.H. (2016). A Questionnaire to Capture Students' Perceptions of Research Integration in Their Courses. *Higher Education*, 71(4), 473–488.

West, M.A. (1987). Role Innovation in the World of Work. *British Journal of Social Psychology*, 26, 305–315.

Zaltman, G., Duncan, R., & Holbek, J. (1973). *Innovations and Organizations*. New York: Wiley.

Zamir, S., & Thomas, M. (2019). Effects of University Teachers' Perceptions, Attitude and Motivation on Their Readiness for the Integration of ICT in Classroom Teaching. *Journal of Education and Educational Development*, 6(2), 308–326.

6 Models and process of curriculum integration and knowledge integration

Introduction

In the context of educational development, integration refers to "interdisciplinary teaching, thematic teaching and synergistic teaching" (Malik & Malik, 2011, p. 99). When applied to teaching, integration is referred as the unification of subjects or disciplines frequently taught in separate academic courses or departments (Harden et al., 1984). When applied to psychology curriculum, knowledge integration refers fully synchronous, integrated transdisciplinary synthesis of Islāmic studies, Islāmic ethical values and Islāmic psychology with psychology sub-disciplines. That is, knowledge from different sources – Qur'ān, Hādīth, Fiqh (Islāmic jurisprudence), Tafsir (exegesis), Seerah (biography of Prophet Muhammad ﷺ) and Islāmic ethics – connects and interrelates with psychology sub-disciplines (abnormal psychology, clinical psychology, counselling psychology, cross-cultural psychology, educational and child psychology, forensic psychology, health psychology, neuropsychology, occupational psychology, sport and exercise psychology, social psychology, etc.). (See Figure 6.1.) The aim of this chapter is to examine the concept

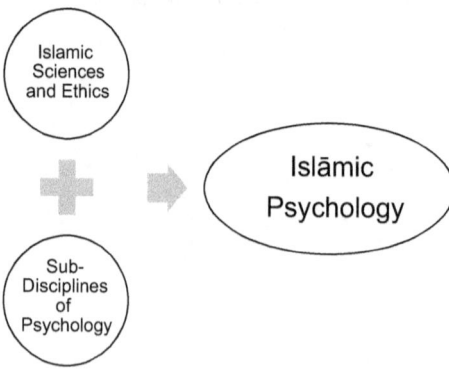

Figure 6.1 Knowledge integration

DOI: 10.4324/9781003329596-6

of integrated curriculum, the educational models and process for integrated curriculum and knowledge integration from an Islāmic perspective. It also presents Rassool's process-driven model of knowledge integration.

Curriculum integration

Most of the definitions of curriculum integration are related to medical education. The International Bureau of Education defines curriculum integration as "the process of combining/articulating learning content and subjects with a view to promoting holistic and comprehensive learning." An integrated curriculum "is generally defined as an educational approach that cuts across and draws on multiple subject areas for learning and instruction. Its purpose is to realistically link various disciplines in the study and exploration of certain aspects of the world" (Adamu, 2003, p. 1). In contrast, Brazee and Capelluti (1995) state that curriculum integration is

> based on a holistic view of learning and recognises the necessity for learners to see the big picture rather than to require learning to be divided into small pieces. Integrative curriculum ignores traditional subject lines while exploring questions that are most relevant to students.

The themes derived from these definitions reflect an aspect of holistic learning, an education approach of teaching and learning activities and combination of disciplines that is Gestalt in nature. In the context of this chapter and book, curriculum integration may be defined as a fully synthesised transdisciplinary delivery of knowledge between psychology sub-disciplines and Islāmic studies and psychology across all the years of an undergraduate or postgraduate psychology programme. The curriculum is organised in such a way that it produces contents of psychological knowledge from an Islāmic perspective. As stated previously, AbuSulayman (1994) defines integration as a union between religious sciences and non-religious sciences. Curriculum integration and knowledge integration is used analogously in this chapter.

Models and process of curriculum integration

Malik and Malik (2011) provided several pointers that can be used to integrate the existing curriculum or develop a new curriculum. It is suggested that "[w]hile the tips are presented in a linear fashion, the process of integration should be seen as an iterative one in which each step (or tip) should inform and affect other steps" (Malik & Malik, 2011, p. 99). These suggestions include training the staff members, deciding on the scope of integration, choosing the level of integration, going for both vertical and horizontal integration, establishing working groups and elucidating their responsibilities, determining learning outcomes, identifying the contents (knowledge, skills and attitudes), creating themes, preparing a comprehensive timetable, selecting assessment methods, communicating with students and staff and committing to re-evaluation and revision. The aims of the faculty development would focus on the purpose of an integrated programme and identify the barriers and the faculty roles and responsibilities in the teaching/learning programme. Malik and Malik (2011) suggest, "To start with, the scope of integration may be limited to only a module or a phase (consisting of several modules). This will help to adapt to a change gradually, it would be less stressful and will provide an opportunity to learn from the experience" (p. 100). It seems that the scope and level of integration may vary from module to module or even within a module and would be dependable upon the aims of the curriculum, the organisational structure, staff and resources and assessment process. The authors recommend the use of both vertical and horizontal integration, curriculum planning and development, communication with students and staff, and commitment to re-evaluation and revision.

Fogarty (1991) describes ten models in the design of curriculum integration. These are the fragmented, connected and nested models (single disciplines); the sequenced, shared, webbed, threaded and integrated models (several disciplines); the immersed model; and the networked model (see Table 6.1). He suggests that these models can be used as prototypes and

Table 6.1 Fogarty's model in the design of curriculum integration

Models	Explanations
Fragmented	Traditionally focuses on a single discipline.
Connected	Focuses on making explicit connections within each subject area.
Nested	Views the curriculum through three-dimensional glasses, targeting multiple dimensions of a lesson.
Sequenced	Views the curriculum through eyeglasses: the lenses are separate but connected by a common frame.
Shared	Views the curriculum through binoculars, bringing two distinct disciplines together into a single focused image.
Webbed	Views the curriculum through a telescope, capturing an entire constellation of disciplines at once.
Threaded	Views the curriculum through a magnifying glass: the "big ideas" are enlarged throughout all content with a meta-curricular approach.
Integrated	Views the curriculum through a kaleidoscope: interdisciplinary topics are rearranged around overlapping concepts and emergent patterns and designs.
Immersed	Views the curriculum through a microscope, in an intensely personal way: it filters all content through the lens of interest and expertise.
Networked	Views the curriculum through a prism, creating multiple dimensions and directions of focus: like a three- or four-way conference call, it provides various avenues of exploration and explanation.

Source: Adapted from Fogarty (1991)

recommends that teachers should design their own model for integrating the curriculum.

In contrast, Harden (2000) provides an 11 steps for a sequential integration strategy used in medical education. This model is based on a continuum of two extremes from isolation to transdisciplinary level: isolation, awareness, harmonisation, nesting, temporal coordination, sharing, correlation, complementary, multidisciplinary, interdisciplinary and transdisciplinary. The first four steps on the ladder focuses on the subjects or disciplines, and the remaining steps emphasise integration across several disciplines. Harden (2000) suggests,

> As one moves up the ladder, there is less emphasis on the role of disciplines, an increasing requirement for a central curriculum, organizational structure and a requirement for greater participation by staff in curriculum discussions and planning. The integration ladder is a useful tool for the medical teacher and can be used as an aid in planning, implementing and evaluating the medical curriculum.
>
> (p. 551)

This model could be as a template to identify at what stage or level a curriculum programme is located and what aspects of the educational programme need further progression. Table 6.2 presents Harden's model of curriculum integration.

Table 6.2 Harden's 11 steps on the integration ladder

Step	Explanations
Isolation	Focuses on organisation of single discipline.
Awareness	Awareness of other disciplines.
Harmonisation	Coordination with other disciplines and adaptation of courses
Nesting	Or infusion. Focuses on content from other courses within own courses.
Temporal coordination	Focuses on similar content covered in parallel across courses.
Sharing	Team teaching. Focuses on common areas of content, or there is a need to include new content in a curriculum.
Correlation	Focuses on integrated teaching and in addition to subject-based teaching.
Complementary	Focuses on contributions of several disciplines on a theme or topic.
Multidisciplinary	Focuses on identification of themes viewed through a multidisciplinary lens. Each discipline maintains its own identity and understanding of the problem.
Interdisciplinary	Focuses on further development of the commonalities across disciplines.
Transdisciplinary	Focuses on the learner's process of constructing meaning from information and experience.

Source: Adapted from Harden (2000) and Brauer and Kristi (2015)

The models described have limitations due to their interpretations by faculty in curriculum integration, mainly in the areas of medical education (Harden's model). Sethi and Khan (2019) have identified several implementation problems with Harden's ladder model of curriculum integration. There is the problem of the misinterpretation of isolation as a form of integration. The authors highlight,

> They [faculty] frequently refer to this being mentioned as the first step in the integration ladder. This becomes problematic when they report subjects taught in isolation as a form of integration when writing self-assessment reports for accreditation purpose, whereas we know that this level involves no integration.
>
> (p. 1)

Sethi and Khan (2019) also pointed out the steps are vague and have overlapping boundaries, level 4 is not for fully integrated overall programme per se, and minimum integration starts at level 5 (temporal coordination), and that institutions jumped the ladder from level 1 to level 7 or even level 9 without passing through other steps. They conclude, "Based on these observations, we believe that there should be no levels of integration as there is no evidence that one level is better than the other" (p. 2). Sethi and Khan (2019) propose three systems of integration: intradepartmental integration (combination of one discipline several disciplines), interdepartmental integration (a few disciplines integrate with each other) and consolidation (disciplines dissolve completely around themes). This model reflects a transdisciplinary level of integration. Bolender et al. (2013) suggest that

> integration is complicated, that getting it right requires careful thinking and the establishment of clear curricular goals, that it can occur while maintaining discipline-based courses and as with any new strategy used, one must determine the gains and losses with respect to the former strategy.
>
> (p. 207)

In most of the medical education programmes, integration has been done on discipline-based courses in the first two years rather than the whole programme. This mode of approach is not relevant or appropriate in psychology as curriculum integration occurs during the duration of the complete course. The emphasis is on the integration across several sub-disciplines of psychology from the beginning to the end of the course programme.

Models and process of knowledge integration: an Islāmic perspective

Knowledge can be integrated through a set of phases, mechanisms or activities based on particular approach or process-driven model. Al-Attas, according to Al Migdadi (2011), suggests two steps to the Islāmised contemporary knowledge. The first is the isolation process, which is where Western-oriented knowledge, culture and civilisation need to be filtered. The second step is that the existing body of knowledge should be integrated with Islāmic elements (Islāmic sciences and ethics) (p. 9). Al-Faruqi proposed a number of steps to achieve the objectives of Islāmisation of knowledge, and these objectives are also relevant and applicable to knowledge integration (see Al-Faruqi, 1989). Ragab (1995) identified three approaches to understand the nature of the process of the methodology in knowledge integration. The first approach is the engagement approach, which is the integration of Islāmic based knowledge with modern social sciences. The second approach, the "disengagement approach" who completely rejects the integration of Islāmic and Western traditions of scholarship. The final approach, the correct approach, is to start with full disengagement with current psychology contents and start from the primary sources of knowledge from the Islāmic categories generated from the Qur'ān and Hadîth. Rajab (1995) argues, "It is dangerous to start from 'modern' preconceptions, because of the natural tendency to superimpose them upon our understanding of Islāmic sources. we have to be wary of the power of ready-made models, for they tend to shape our perceptions, wittingly or unwittingly" (p. 116). Rajab (1999) goes on to suggest that modern

[s]ocial scientists can instantly start the process of utilisation of the Qur'ān and Sunnah, and the Islāmic legacy derived from them immediately. It is my contention that specific social science disciplines (especially psychology, sociology, anthropology, education, communication, social work, and psychotherapy) can very productively use Islāmic (*Shari'ah*) sciences at their current level of development.

(p. 34)

Nasr (2010) provides an alternative solution to the Islāmisation of knowledge and presents some fundamental principles in shifting the paradigm of knowledge. He suggested six major steps in his model that could be employed by those who are willing to engage in the process. These steps include the mastering the field of knowledge (psychology) in order to identify the contradictory and the consensual points; mastering the philosophy and methodologies of modern science; being well-versed with Muslim intellectual tradition; effectively using language as it plays a significant role in knowledge dissemination; the sieving stage, as the Islāmic world needs to utilise all its resources to know this science (psychology) in depth and breadth and in its relation to religion, philosophy and social forces, to enable critical review of its the premises and conclusions from an Islāmic perspective; and Islāmic scholars in the course of Islāmisation process must create a new paradigm of knowledge from Islāmic sources.

Malkawi (2015) suggests, "The process of epistemological integration has two dimensions: a productive, scientific, creative dimension, and a consumptive,

90 Models and process of curriculum and knowledge integration

pedagogical, applied dimension" (p. 5). In its productive dimension, integration of knowledge is a form of intellectual creativity which requires special skills. In this phase, it is important "to deconstruct the issue at hand, identify its elements, and understand the mechanism by which it operates and its underlying theoretical assumptions or premises" (p. 5). Part of that dimension is the constructive process in order to produce a new epistemological integration. As for the consumptive dimension of epistemological integration, it has to do with communicating this amalgam of knowledge to others. Malkawi (2015) provides the difference between the productive and the consumptive dimensions of epistemological integration. This

> might be likened to the difference between the physicist who discovers a given natural law or the technologist who develops an instrument or machine based on this law, and the technician who works in a factory in which this instrument or machine is used.
>
> (p. 5)

Rassool (2022) proposes six different knowledge integration mechanisms for the decolonisation of psychology knowledge and a process-driven model of curriculum integration.

Mechanism of knowledge integration

Rassool (2022) has developed a model of knowledge integration for the psychology discipline based on (1) planning, (2) mastering, (3) deconstructing, (4) curriculum mapping, (5) scope/level of integration with Islāmic studies/psychology, and (6) knowledge transfer (see Figure 6.2). These mechanisms are operated in a systematic, logical development in the context of psychology knowledge. The first mechanism for knowledge integration is the planning and setting up on working groups. A working group will need to be set up, and each sub-discipline of psychology should have its own Psychology Sub-discipline Integration Team (PSIT), under the direction of a Faculty Capacity Development Integration Committee (FCDIC). Each working group will have its terms of reference and the responsibilities of the members. The second mechanism is mastering. Mastering is having a sound understanding of the whole psychology curriculum. It is valuable at this stage to assess the level of the mastering of the curriculum content of the lecturers and selecting those with sound knowledge of the theories, methodologies and research findings of the sub-discipline of psychology. In addition, the assessment of current knowledge of Islāmic studies – Qur'ān, Hādīth, *Tafsir* (exegesis), *Seerah* (the Prophet Muhammad's biography), *Fiqh* (Islāmic jurisprudence), Islāmic ethics and Islāmic civilisation – of lecturers needs to be established. In the absence of experts in Islāmic studies in the Department of Psychology, expertise should be sought from the Department of Islāmic Studies or from an

Models and process of curriculum and knowledge integration 91

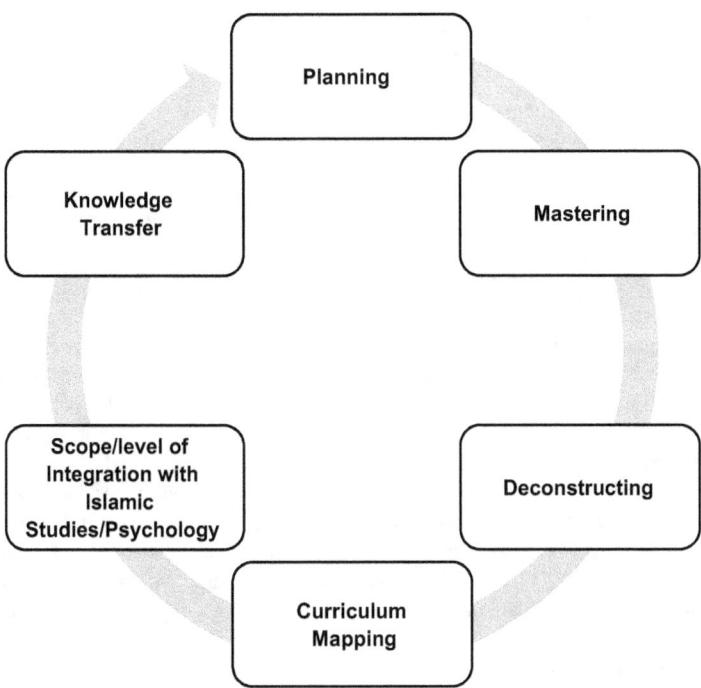

Figure 6.2 Knowledge integration mechanisms

external expert. At this stage, the question relates to what the accepted canon of knowledge in psychology sub-disciplines is. Should Islāmic psychology even be a distinct discipline on its own?

Having identified that the psychology curriculum is oriented towards Eurocentric approach, how do we go about deconstructing it? Deconstructing the curriculum is to probe the current canon of psychology, to examine and reflect on the contents of the psychology modules that need modification so that knowledge integration can be implemented. How might our course content be reconceptualised in order to reflect wider Islāmic perspectives? When looking at the historical and evolution of psychology as discipline, can we find other sources of knowledge? How might psychology be taught in a way that promotes narratives from both Western and Islāmic cultural norms and traditions? How can we provide our students access to previously unheard perspectives of psychology in the development of psychology by classical Islāmic scholars? This mechanism is to broaden the knowledge production landscape for each psychology sub-discipline module with Islāmic studies, Islāmic ethics and Islāmic psychology. Deconstructing the curriculum also has another function in the provision of understanding of the importance of constructive alignment of the planned and lived curriculum.

Another mechanism is the use of curriculum mapping. This is a reflective process that helps educators to identify the contents, methods and how learning outcomes are assessed. Curriculum maps are designed to produce concepts maps mostly done that consist of a table or matrix. Curriculum mapping is an important task to show the path of good practice in teaching and learning activities. Their use is in the proper constructive alignment of aims, learning outcomes, instructional support materials, summative and formative assessments, and finally the scheme of study. It is critical for constructive alignment to start with the outcomes in mind, referred as backwards design (Wiggins & McTighe, 2005). The curriculum mapping steps, which is critical to ensure alignment from beginning to end, include writing aims (course or module); writing learning outcomes (skills, knowledge or attitudes you want the students to achieve by the end of the module or course); identifying and preparing course materials and resources (textbook, reading materials, open educational resources, videos and web resources); planning for formative assessment (informal, graded or ungraded but with no effect on overall formal grading); and summative assessment (formal, with grades having an effect on overall grading). Once you have completed the planning, you need to ensure that all the steps are aligned with all previous steps. An important function of the curriculum maps is to provide structure and consistency by the process of curriculum sequencing. Sequencing of courses in the curriculum involves the arrangement of course contents in a specific order. Prerequisites for one module in a sub-discipline of psychology may include the learning outcomes achieved in a previous module. This is about the mapping out the knowledge, skills and contents to indicate the level of progression for students to achieve from the stage of apprenticeship (basic knowledge and skills) to mastery. Students' increasing mastery is supported by repeated exposure to and practice of knowledge, skills and abilities through a variety of methodologies of teaching and learning activities. Mapping of themes "enables teachers to meaningfully link different disciplines so that students will see the 'big' picture and appreciate the relevance of learning to their future [clinical] practice" (Malik & Malik, 2011, p. 101).

Decision needs to be made on the scope and level of integration. The scope and level of integration is less restrictive for a new course or module. However, for an existing psychology course, it would be possible or practical to change all the contents of the course due to the educational policy of accrediting and validating bodies. In an undergraduate or postgraduate course in psychology, the scope of integration may be limited to a few modules, as identified by the concept mapping and sequencing process. This would provide valuable feedback for further development in curriculum integration. The level of integration has been represented as a continuum with full integration in one end and discipline-based teaching on another (Harden et al., 1984). Fogarty (1991) describes 10 levels of curriculum integration, and Harden (2000) describes 11 steps in the level of integration from isolation to transdisciplinary. The transdisciplinary curriculum would be the most effective method and, most likely, the easiest pathway to implement knowledge integration of Islāmic studies and Islāmic psychology in psychology knowledge. In this context, psychology will be totally integrated, if appropriate and relevant, with Islāmic studies and Islāmic psychology. It is worth pointing out that although constructive alignment of the curriculum and knowledge integration are ideal in theory, they "are difficult to implement due to different weightage and time allotments of various subjects. Lack of proper interdisciplinary coordination leads to difficulty in framing a timetable for integrated teaching sessions.

Rassool's process-driven model of curriculum integration

Figure 6.3 illustrates Rassool's process-driven model of knowledge integration for the psychology curriculum. The starting point is the process of undertaking a training needs analysis (TNA). A TNA helps to pinpoint which areas need addressing within the academic institution or Department of Psychology. It will give you a clear view of what skills and experience that are needed for knowledge and curriculum integration to get ahead and which of those are missing at the moment. It allows the creation of a learning and development

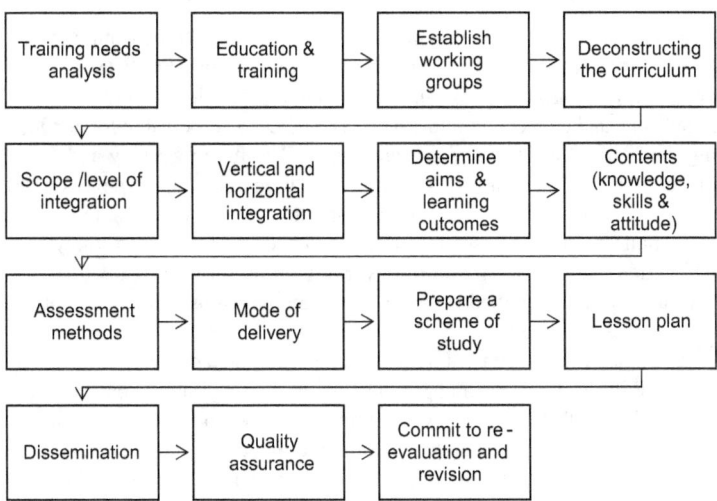

Figure 6.3 Rassool's process-driven model of knowledge integration for the psychology curriculum

94 *Models and process of curriculum and knowledge integration*

plan based on the needs of the employees. For example, the TNA will take a bird's eye view of the psychology lectures' knowledge based in Islāmic sciences and Islāmic psychology. Conducting a TNA before setting up an education and training plan is a crucial step to developing more effective training materials and capturing the best use of the staff resources. The TNA methods that are appropriate for this kind of analysis include questionnaires, observation and interviews. The findings from the TNA will enable the development of an education and training plan. The aims of the education programmes are to achieve the following:

- Understand the limitations of secular psychology
- Have an awareness of the rationale and aims for integrating Islāmic psychology and Islāmic studies in psychology
- Acquire sound knowledge of Islāmic psychology and Islāmic studies
- Examine the why, what and how of integrating Islāmic psychology and Islāmic sciences in the undergraduate and postgraduate psychology curricula
- Familiarise with the aims and purpose of an integrated curriculum programme
- Identify the local barriers and facilitators of knowledge integration
- Develop skills in knowledge integration of Islāmic psychology and Islāmic studies in teaching practices
- Appreciate and apply he university's values in personal and professional life
- Provide continuous professional development in Islāmic psychology and Islāmic studies

For example, in the Department of Psychology at Riphah International University, a Faculty Capacity Development Programme (FCDP) was developed for the purpose of the Islāmisation of psychology knowledge and knowledge and curriculum integration. The FCDP is responsible for conducting the TNA in Islāmic sciences and ethics. The future strategy and future planning of the FCDP include the implementation of a focus group to review progress of Islāmisation of knowledge or knowledge integration, the implementation of a monthly seminar and a series of workshops on knowledge integration, and the setting up of a working group for writing textbooks on various subjects in applied psychology and on the philosophical foundations of Islāmic psychology.

It is essential to set up different working groups and define their roles and responsibilities. One working group is the Psychology Sub-disciplines Integration Team (PSIT), which works under the direction and supervision of the Faculty Capacity Development Integration Committee (FCDIC). Each working group will have its terms of reference and the responsibilities of the memberships. Ideally, both teams should have memberships from both departments of psychology (clinicians and academics) and Islāmic studies. Both the deconstruction and the scope and level of integration have

Models and process of curriculum and knowledge integration 95

been examined in previous section. However, within the scope and level of integration, a transdisciplinary curriculum (Stember, 1991) would be most appropriate. That would encompass, organise, synthesise and integrate all knowledge from the psychology and Islāmic disciplines with the function of producing new knowledge. There is also the adoption of vertical integration and horizontal integration. In this context, Rassool's vertical and horizontal integrated, embedded curriculum model (Rassool, 2020) will be used as framework. Determining aims and learning outcomes is part of the process of curriculum development. Aims are general statements of intent, and intended learning outcomes are specific statements formulated to identify the knowledge, skills and attitudes to be achieved in a particular module. The use of Bloom's taxonomy of educational objectives (Anderson & Krathwohl, 2001) is useful here. The contents of the scheme of study are based on the intended learning outcomes and are based on the acquisition of knowledge, skills to be learned and attitudes to be developed. Each sub-discipline of psychology integrated with Islāmic studies and psychology is to be mapped for their curriculum content. A knowledge integrated assessment is essential to reflect an integrated curriculum based on a diversity of tools of assessment. This leads to the delivery of teaching and learning activities based on the learning outcomes and curriculum contents. A scheme of studies is prepared by the working group to determine the sequence of teaching/learning sessions. The flow of the topics should be logical, and each new topic should build on prior learning. Lesson plans are prepared by the subject specialist showing knowledge integration. The dissemination of schemes of study and samples of lesson plans should be disseminated to all concerned. Quality assurance for the evaluation of knowledge and curriculum integration implies controlling and raising the quality of education and ensuring that minimum standards of integration are achieved. There is the assessment of teaching and learning activities (students, internal and external faculty, external examiner). There should also be a commitment for re-evaluation and revision. Re-evaluation and remodification of the psychology curriculum would be based on feedback from quality assurance. The main focus is to evaluate whether there has been knowledge transfer in teaching practices. It is the responsibility of the Faculty Integration Committee (FIC) to implement changes, if appropriate.

Characteristics of effective knowledge integration

According to Grant (1996), there are three main characteristics which make the integration of knowledge effective:

- The efficiency of integration
- The scope of integration
- The flexibility of integration

These characteristics will be examined in the context of knowledge integration in the psychology curriculum. When discussing the efficiency of integration, there is a need considering the extent to which the academic institutions or departments of psychology are capable of implementing knowledge integration in the psychology curriculum and in its application in teaching practices. The efficiency at which academic institutions or departments of psychology integrate knowledge will depend on the role adequacy and role legitimacy of the lecturers (Rassool, 2020, 2021) and organisational culture supporting the knowledge integration enterprise. The scope of integration concerns the breadth of knowledge of sub-disciplines of psychology, Islāmic studies and psychology that can be harnessed from lecturers through the integration process. Specialist knowledge in the area of Islāmic studies, including the Qur'ān and Hadîth and the works of classical scholars and modern thinkers, brings advantage to the academic institutions. Lastly, the flexibility of the integration depends on the capabilities of the integration mechanisms to integrate new knowledge and reconstructing the existing curriculum.

Anticipated challenges in curriculum integration

Like any innovation, the process of integration is bound to meet several challenges and impediments in its acceptance and implementation. There is a major challenge in changing the convictions of our scholars, academicians, clinicians and students to instil Islāmic studies and psychology in academia and clinical and teaching practices. This is no meagre task as there is the emerging "role conflict for some Muslim psychologists in the context of being pulled between being a Muslim and being a 'secular' psychologist" (Rassool, 2022, pp. 229–230). In fact, some may even explicitly reject such inclusion because of their secular attitudes, on the mixing of psychology based on Western scientific paradigm with Islāmic theology.

On a global level, many educational institutions face enormous challenges in the integration of Islāmic sciences in undergraduate, postgraduate and professional development courses. Rassool (2021) suggests,

> In most countries, due to institutional and professional regulations in psychology, counselling and psychotherapy courses, educational institutions are restricted in their attempt to integrate Islāmic studies and psychology in their curricula. Perhaps, that is the rationale behind adopting the "Sprinkle or Bolt-on" approaches in their curriculum.
>
> (p. 602)

Against this background, we are faced with other challenges to overcome. Muslim psychology teachers are generally trained to teach sub-disciplines of secular psychology, and most have limited knowledge Islāmic studies and psychology. There is also the issue of attitude, knowledge, skills and commitment

(Islāmic commitment) of Muslim psychologists. This Islāmic commitment incorporates the evaluation of whether Muslim psychologists have adequate knowledge, training and experience to decolonise their psychology knowledge. It is plausible that both role adequacy and role legitimacy may constitute important predictors of Muslim psychologists' willingness to engage in the knowledge and curriculum integration. Rassool (2021) has also identified problems and issues related to role legitimacy, role adequacy and role conflict. These emerging issues have been addressed in the previous chapter.

Conclusion

Knowledge integration is an ongoing process that occurs at many levels; it is a journey of transformation for academic institutions, institutional structures, lecturers, researchers and students. There is no "one size fits all" blueprint for knowledge and curriculum integration for all disciplines as it may involve lots of different approaches and processes: it is important to highlight that an integrated curriculum may look very different for the sub-disciplines of psychology, because the curriculum or knowledge integration may not be possible for certain themes. However, contextual factors, organisational structure, organisational support, resource implications and policy commitment of the Islāmisation of the social sciences, including psychology, need to be addressed at the institutional level. Rassool (2020) suggests, "If there is no sense of urgency and low expectations within an organisation culture, this may inhibit the emergence of Islāmic psychology as a discipline" (p. 494). Above all, we should have an awareness that knowledge integration is not the sole property of Muslim psychologists. The solutions lie in all of us. We should be producers of knowledge rather than consumers of knowledge.

Bibliography

AbuSulayman. A. (1994). *Islamisation: Reforming contemporary knowledge*. Herndon-VA: IIIT.

Adamu, A.U. (2003). *The Concept of Curriculum Integration: Its Meaning, Scope and Modalities*. https://auadamu.com/phocadownload/Conference_Presentations/Education_Presentations/2003%20Curriculum%20Integration.pdf#:~:text=An%20integrated%20curriculum%20is%20generally%20defined%20as%20an,a%20noted%20proponent%20of%20integrated%20curriculum%2C%20explains%20that%3As (accessed 26 September 2022).

Al-Faruqi, I.R. (1989). *Islāmisation of Knowledge-General Principles and Work Plan*. Herndon, VA: International Institute of Islāmic Thought.

Al Migdadi, M.H. (2011). Issues in Islāmization of Knowledge, Man and Education. *Revue Académique des Sciences Humaines et Sociales*, 7, 11.

Anderson, L.W., & Krathwohl, D.R. (2001). *A Taxonomy for Learning, Teaching, and Assessing: A Revision of Bloom's Taxonomy of Educational Objectives*. New York: Longman.

Bolender, D.L., Ettarh, R., Jerrett, D.P., & Laherty, R.F. (2013). Curriculum Integration = Course Disintegration: What Does This Mean for Anatomy? *Anatomical Science Education*, 6(3), 205–208.

Brauer, D.G., & Ferguson, K.J. (2015). The Integrated Curriculum in Medical Education: AMEE Guide No. 96. *Medical Teacher*, 37, 312–322.

Brazee, E.N., & Capelluti, J. (1995). *Dissolving Boundaries: Toward an Integrative Curriculum*. Columbus, OH: National Middle States Association.

Fogarty, R. (1991). *How to Integrate Curricula*. Palatine, IL: IRI/Skylight Training and Publishing, Inc.

Grant, R.M. (1996). Prospering in Dynamically Competitive Environments: Organizational Capability as Knowledge Integration. *Organization Science*, 7(4), 375–387.

Harden, R.M. (2000). The Integration Ladder: A Tool for Curriculum Planning and Evaluation. *Medical Education*, 34, 551–557.

Harden, R.M., Sowden, S., & Dunn, W.R. (1984). Some Educational Strategies in Curriculum Development: The SPICES Model. ASME Medical Education Booklet Number 18. *Medical Education*, 18, 284–297.

International Bureau of Education. *Curriculum Integration*. Geneva, Switzerland: UNESCO. www.ibe.unesco.org/en/glossary-curriculum-terminology/c/curriculum-integration (accessed 26 September 2022).

Malik, A.S., & Malik, R.H. (2011). Twelve Tips for Developing an Integrated Curriculum. *Medical Teacher*, 33(2), 99–104.

Malkawi, F.H. (2015). *Epistemological Integration: Essentials of an Islāmic Methodology* (Translated from Arabic by Nancy Roberts and Abridged by Wanda Krause). Herndon, VA: International Institute of Islāmic Thought (IIIT).

Nasr, S.H. (2010). *Islāmic Life and Thought*. Kuala Lumpur: Islāmic Book Trust.

Patel, M., & Shah, H.D. (2020). Alignment and Integration in Competency-Based Medical Education Curriculum: An Overview. *Indian Journal of Physiology and Pharmacology*, 64(Suppl_1), S13–S15.

Ragab, I.A. (1995). On the Nature and Scope of the Islāmization Process: Towards Conceptual Clarification. *Intellectual Discourse*, 3(2), 113–122.

Ragab, I.A. (1999). On the Methodology of Islāmizing the Social Sciences. *Intellectual Discourse*, 7(1), 27–52.

Rassool, G.H. (2020). Cognitive Restructuring of Psychology: The Case for a Vertical and Horizontal Integrated, Embedded Curriculum Model for Islāmic Psychology. *Islāmic Studies*, 59(4), 477–494.

Rassool, G.H. (2021). Decolonising Psychology and its (Dis) Contents. In G.H. Rassool (Ed.), *Islāmic Psychology: Human Behaviour and Experiences from an Islāmic Perspective*. Oxford: Routledge, pp. 583–601.

Rassool, G.H. (2022). *Mechanism of Knowledge Integration and Process-Driven Model of Curriculum Integration*. Unpublished Paper.

Sethi, A., & Khan, R.A. (2019). Curriculum integration: From Ladder to Ludo. *Medical Teacher*. https://doi.org/10.1080/0142159X.2019.1707176.

Stember, M. (1991). Advancing the Social Sciences Through the Interdisciplinary Enterprise. *The Social Science Journal*, 28(1), 1–14.

Wiggins, G., & McTighe, J. (2005). *Understanding by Design* (2nd ed.). Alexandria, VA: ASCD.

7 Rassool's vertical and horizontal integrated embedded curriculum model of Islāmic psychology

Introduction

Educational development in Islāmic psychology is a slapdash process, and there is a dearth of literature relating to curriculum approaches, development and evaluation of educational programmes. The review undertaken by Haque et al. (2016) of the state of Islām and psychology publications over a period of ten years (2006–2015) fails to identify one single paper on educational development in Islāmic psychology. For an emerging discipline with comprehensive theoretical foundations on models of the soul and therapeutic interventions, there seems to be a dissonance between educational development and clinical practice (Rassool, 2019). There is an assumption that one of the factors that has inhibited the integration of Islāmic psychology and ethics in psychology curriculum is the lack of an educational conceptual framework in Islāmic psychology. The focus of this chapter is to examine the curriculum approaches in Islāmic psychology and present an educational conceptual framework in the form of a vertical and horizontal integrated, embedded curriculum model.

Conceptual educational framework for decolonising psychology knowledge

The development of this conceptual educational framework for the integration of Islāmic ethics and studies in the psychology programme is an amalgam of Al-Faruqi's (1988) framework, which is based on five principles of Islām, presented in Figure 7.1. These include oneness of God, unity of creation, unity of truth, unity of life and unity of humanity. From these principles, according to Al-Faruqi, scholars who are responsible for the development of the Islāmisation process need be an expert in modern science and Islāmic knowledge of those fields. In the context of psychology, academics need to have psychology knowledge and knowledge of Islāmic studies and ethics. Al-Faruqi's framework is used to produce Rassool's framework for the development of Islāmic psychology.

DOI: 10.4324/9781003329596-7

100 Rassool's vertical and horizontal integrated curriculum

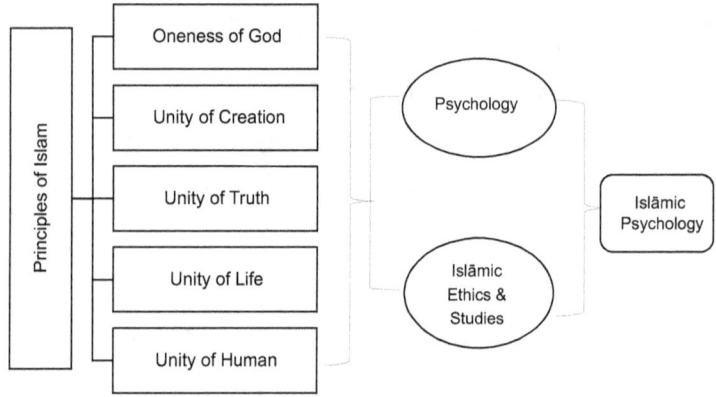

Figure 7.1 Rassool's framework for Islāmisation of knowledge

In contrast, Berghout (2011) focused on a model of learning approach to enhance the process of Islāmisation within tertiary education and its evaluation (see Figure 7.2). His system is a process model that includes an input, process, output and feedback. In the input phase, "the Islāmic worldview and values, Islāmic environments, Islāmic curriculum and Islāmic guidelines, policies and principles of learning are integrated" (p. 24). The process includes the integration of Islāmic worldview leading to appropriate learning and teaching activities. The output "should reflect the Islāmic perspective in the form of Islāmised individuals, research outputs, services, and Islāmised products" (p. 24). Feedback is part of the evaluation of teaching and learning activities and interdependent aspects of the educative process. This involves the monitoring, implementation and evaluation of the Islāmisation programme to determine the effectiveness of teaching methodologies, learning activities, instructional materials and other elements affecting the teaching-learning process with the end in view of improvement. It has been suggested that Berghout's Islāmisation of science framework focus on three domains of educational taxonomy: cognitive, affective and psychomotor skills (Madani, 2016).

The main focus of the educational taxonomy is on the affective domain because Berghout (2011) maintains that

> from an Islāmic perspective the question of affective domain and values is crucial not only in the learning process and knowledge creation and dissemination, but also in the development of the well-being and personality of the teacher and learner as well.
>
> (p. 31)

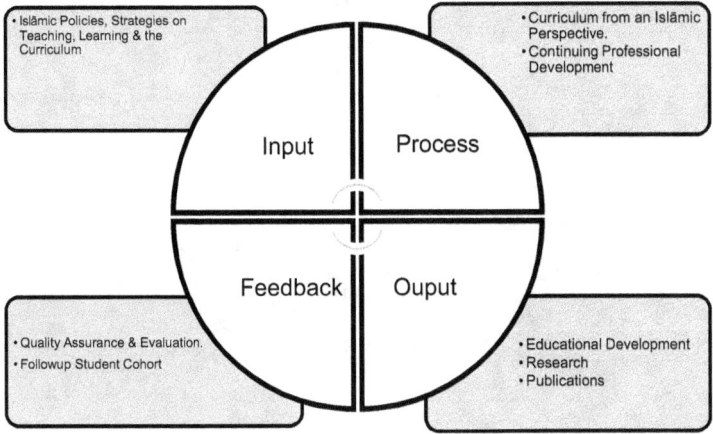

Figure 7.2 Berghout's model of Islāmisation
Source: Adapted from Berghout (2011)

This means the teaching of ethical and moral values are accorded significant importance.

Rassool's curriculum model of knowledge integration is a modification of previous model (Rassool, 2020, 2021a) based on Al-Faruqi's five principles of Islām and the Berghout's model of learning. The model identifies core components and the interrelationships between these components in the development of effective educational programmes. The conceptual framework is presented in Figure 7.3. The philosophy of education projected by Al-Farūqī was constructed on the worldview of *Tawhîd* rooted on Islāmic vision of reality and truth. The *Tawhîd* paradigm takes its name from the core Islāmic concept of *Tawhîd* (unicity of God, the doctrine of God's incomparability). Al-Farūqī (1992) suggests that the *Tawhîd* paradigm "manifests the readiness and willingness to fulfil the Divine trust (*al-amanah*) and obligatory duties (*al-fara'id*) that are accompanied by the Divine guidance and human unique capability" (Qur'ān Hud 11:6; Az-Zumar 39:41) (p. 5). What Al-Farūqī was proposing is having a holistic approach to the development of educational programmes that seek to integrate the fundamental element of revealed and scientific knowledge.

Berghout's system approach provides a holistic view of the stages in the Islāmisation of knowledge. His approach synthesises the different stages of organisational, policy and educational development and converges them into an adaptive and dynamic entity. However, some of the model's limitations

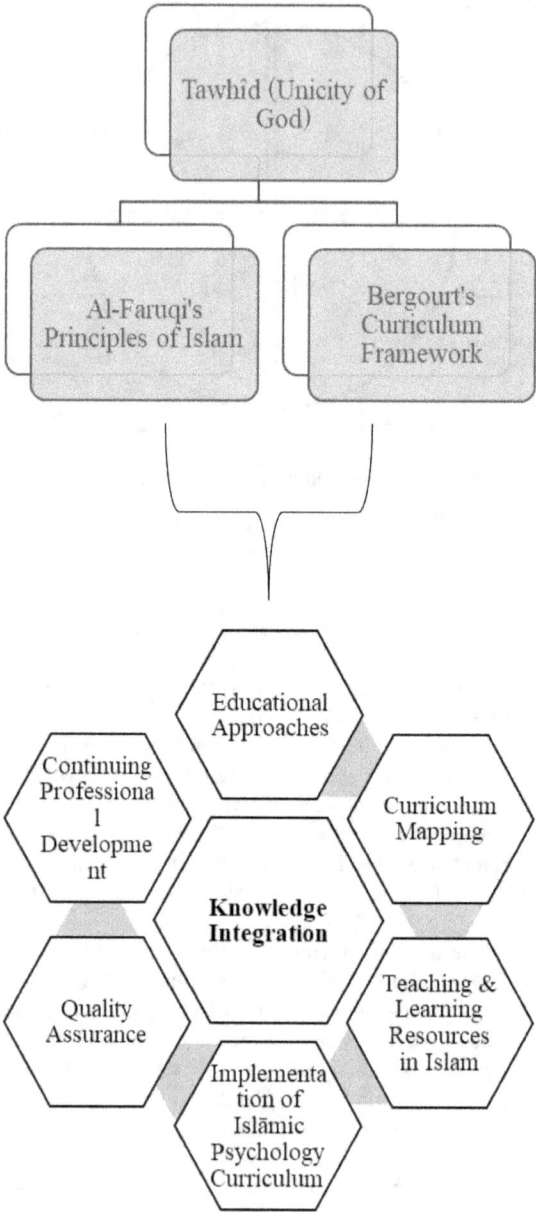

Figure 7.3 Rassool's proposed educational conceptual framework for knowledge integration in psychology based on the *Tawhîd* paradigm

include being too theoretical in approach, and in practice, there are external constraints that may inhibit the interdependence of the different stages. It may also not be applicable to diverse, heterogeneous educational institutions in Muslim countries. Despite its limitations, it is a useful tool in the development, integration, implementation and evaluation in integrating Islāmic sciences and ethics in psychology.

Rassool's vertical and horizontal integrated, embedded curriculum model of Islāmic psychology

In this framework, Al-Farūqī's (1992) approach in the Islāmisation of knowledge has been utilised as the guiding philosophical principles, whereas Berghout's (2011) system approach to education forms the basis of the organisational and curriculum development. In addition, a model of curriculum development that is being proposed attempts to show how to integrate Islāmic psychology and Islāmic ethics in the undergraduate and postgraduate psychology curriculum. The model is a vertically and horizontally integrated, embedded curriculum and is presented in Figure 7.4. The two dimensions of the model are the horizontal and vertical integration. These two dimensions are key aspects in curriculum design and development. According to Daniel (2014), "Vertical organisation (sequence, continuity-deepening of knowledge) deals with the longitudinal arrangement of the design components. Horizontal organisation (scope, integration-widening of knowledge) deals with the side-by-side arrangement of the components in the curriculum." In this model, the horizontal axis includes integration and scope.

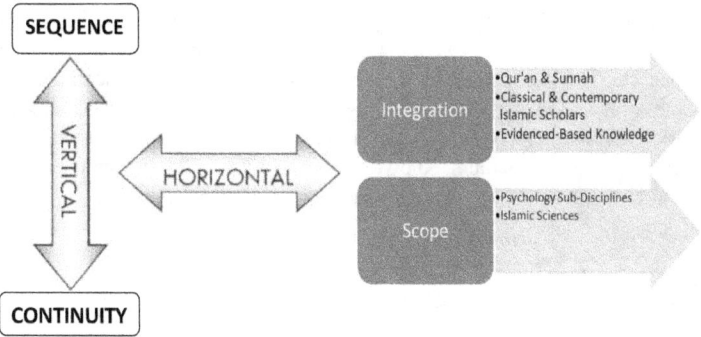

Figure 7.4 Rassool's vertical and horizontal integration curriculum approach
Source: Rassool (2020)

Horizontal axis

Horizontal integration refers to the relations among various contents, topics and themes involving all domains of knowledge. That is a kind of integration between parallel disciplines emanating from both evidenced-based knowledge, the classical and contemporary work of Islāmic scholars and knowledge based on the Qur'ān and Hadîth. Horizontal integration may also mean the integration of basic concepts from one discipline into another, using a transdisciplinary model. Horizontal integration is integration between parallel disciplines, such anatomy, physiology, endocrinology, health, disease, psychology and Islāmic studies. For example, sub-disciplines of psychology, such as health psychology, certain basic themes, including diabetes, cardiovascular disease, hypertension, obesity, prophetic medicine, health and fasting in Ramadan, bio-psychosocial and spiritual benefits of fasting, physiological and psychological changes during fasting, nutrition, and dealing with anger and stress from an Islāmic perspective, among others, are taught in the same phase of the curriculum. Another example is the course of the biological bases of behaviour, where the themes that may be included are, for example, the Islāmic contribution to biological psychology, Islāmic epistemology, evolutionary psychology from an Islāmic perspective, role of the soul in the nature versus nurture, determinants of human behaviours, bio-ethics from an Islāmic perspective, hearing as a gift (Qur'ān 23:78), creation of hearing in the foetus comes before sight (Qur'ān 76:2), hearing as a constant link with the outside world (Qur'ān 18:11), hearing as a blessing and a responsibility, and the study on how Qur'ānic recitation promote mental health (Owens et al., 2022).

Scope: This dimension focused on the breadth and depth of the curriculum content. The horizontal curriculum integrates knowledge across different classes or sub-disciplines of psychology. These disciplines or sub-disciplines include life-span development, child psychology, social psychology, biological bases of behaviour, cognitive psychology, abnormal psychology, history and philosophy of Islāmic psychology, psychology of religion, health psychology, community psychology Islāmic philosophy, Islāmic sciences, Islāmic ethics, etc. The sub-disciplines would be based on the aims and learning outcomes of the complete educational programme. In addition, the psychological works of prominent Islāmic classical and contemporary scholars would be integrated in the curriculum. Knowledge of the scope of the curriculum assists in the selection of methodology of teaching and learning experiences.

Vertical axis

Vertical integration is referred as the "organization of contents according to the sequence and continuity of learning within a given knowledge domain or subject over time (vertical articulation to improve coherence)" (International Bureau of Education, 2020). What is important in this axis is the role of sequence and continuity in the design, organisation and development of the curriculum elements. In vertical integration, the educational contents tend to be organised with regard to the sequence and continuity of learning and teaching processes.

The identification of the sequence of the learning experiences is a building block for the transition from basic to more advanced knowledge (cognitive) and skills (psychomotor). For example, in an undergraduate course, Introduction to Psychology and Introduction to Islāmic Psychology modules would be a prerequisite for subsequent more advanced courses in Islāmic psychology. Both modules will introduce the fundamental principles of psychology and Islāmic psychology and the major subjects of psychological inquiry. In relation to the skills domain of the educational programme, vertical integration relates to the process of actively involving the undergraduate students in the development of skills. For example, in an Islāmic psychotherapy module, the development of the therapist has most often been seen as a matter of individual and personal development – that is, moving on a progression of novice, advanced beginner, competent, proficient and, finally, expert or advanced practitioner (vertical skills development). Vertical skills development refers to training trainee psychotherapists to handle increased responsibilities. In a vertical curriculum, what is learned during the novice phase prepares the trainee counsellors for the next phase. In this approach, basic skills and knowledge are both developed and reinforced as other more micro-skills elements are introduced in the educational programme. According to this perspective, the process of curriculum organisation represents an effort to enhance the scope, integration, sequence and continuity of the Islāmic psychology and counselling curriculum. To gain the maximum benefit, one needs to integrate the curriculum both horizontally and vertically. The next chapter provides the modules' contents of an undergraduate course in psychology based on Rassool's vertically and horizontally integrated curriculum's model of knowledge integration.

Bibliography

Al-Faruqi, I.R. (1988). Islāmization of Knowledge: Problems, Principles and Prospective. In *Proceedings & Selected Papers of the Second Conference on Islāmization of Knowledge, 1402 AH /1982 AD*. Herndon, VA: International Institute of Islāmic Thought, pp. 13–64.
Al-Faruqi, I.R. (1992). *Al Tawhid: Its Implications for Thought and Life*. Herndon, Virginia: International Institute of Islamic Thought.
Berghout, A. (2011). Values and Education within the Framework of Islāmisation of Knowledge. In W.F. Faris et al. (Eds.), *Ethics and Values in Science and Technology*. International Islāmic University Malaysia. Kuala Lumpur: IIUM Press, pp. 3–15.
Daniel, E. (2014). "INLS 242: Curriculum Issues and the School Library Media Specialist," *Curriculum Notes*. Retrieved on 17 May 2023 from https://ils.unc.edu/daniel/242/CurrNotes.html.

Haque, A., Khan, F., Keshavarzi, H., & Rothman, A.E. (2016). Integrating Islāmic Traditions in Modern Psychology: Research Trends in Last Ten Years. *Journal of Muslim Mental Health*, 10(1), 75–100.

International Bureau of Education. (2020). *Vertical and Horizontal Articulation* (of the curriculum). www.ibe.unesco.org/en/glossary-curriculum-terminology/v/vertical-and-horizontal-articulation-curriculum (accessed 27 September 2022).

Madani, R.H. (2016). Islāmization of Science. *International Journal of Islāmic Thought*, 9(1), 51–63.

Owens, J., Rassool, G.H., Bernstein, J., Latif, S., & Aboul-Enein, B. (2022). Interventions Using the Qur'ān to Protect and Promote Mental Health: A Systematic Scoping Review. *Inplasy Protocol*, 202270065. http://doi.org/10.37766/inplasy2022.7.0065.

Rassool, G.H. (2019). *Sharing the Vision: The Cognitive Restructuring of Islāmisation of Knowledge in Psychology*. Keynote Presentation at the International Conference on Islāmic Perspectives In Modern Psychology (IPMO 2019) (24th to September 2019). Lahore, Pakistan.

Rassool, G.H. (2020). Cognitive Restructuring of Psychology: The Case for a Vertical and Horizontal Integrated, Embedded Curriculum Model for Islāmic Psychology. *Islāmic Studies*, 59(4), 477–494.

Rassool, G.H. (2021a). Decolonising Psychology and its (Dis) Contents. In G.H. Rassool (Ed.), *Islāmic Psychology: Human Behaviour and Experiences from an Islāmic Perspective*. Oxford: Routledge, pp. 583–601.

Rassool, G.H. (2021b). *Islāmic Psychology: Human Behaviour and Experiences from an Islāmic Perspective*. Oxford: Routledge.

8 Course scheme in Islāmic psychology
Knowledge integration

Introduction

This is a sample course scheme for an Introduction to Psychology course as part of an undergraduate psychology curriculum. A course scheme is similar to a scheme of work, which is a "plan setting out how the programme of study, syllabus, or curriculum will be translated into teaching and learning activities, including the sequencing of content, the amount of time spent on each topic, and how the specified learning objectives will be assessed" (Oxford Reference, 2022). A course scheme is taken from the curriculum, and it focuses on how the curriculum will be converted into teaching and learning activities. The contents of the teaching and learning activities reflect knowledge integration of both evidenced-based psychology and Islāmic psychology.

Course Scheme

Introduction To Psychology

1. Course Title	Introduction to Psychology	
2. Code	xxxx	
3. Programme	Bachelor of Science Degree in Psychology – BS	
4. Department	Psychology	
5. Course Credits	3	
6. Year of Study	1	
7. Semester	1	
8. Duration	16 weeks	
9. Module Context	X Core	Elective
10. Description, Purpose and Aim(s)	**Description:** Psychologists study behaviour at different levels of explanation, ranging from lower biological levels to higher social and cultural levels and spiritual dimensions. The same behaviours can be studied and explained within psychology at different levels of explanation. **Purpose and Aims:** The main aims are to introduce an understanding of the different areas of psychology and explore some of the concepts, theories and approaches in psychology from secular and Islāmic perspectives.	

(Continued)

Course scheme in Islāmic psychology

Introduction To Psychology

11. **Intended Learning Outcomes**	Upon completion of this, students should be able to: Define psychology and Islāmic psychology. Compare and contrast secular psychology and Islāmic psychology. Compare and contrast the sources of knowledge used for the Islāmic and secular perspectives. Discuss the issues and problems associated with secular psychology. Identify the complex relationship between psychology and religion. Critically evaluate different theoretical approaches to the study of psychology. Explain the mechanism of biological components and its behavioural effects on human beings. Compare secular and Islāmic approaches to the study of human nature and personality. Outline the stages of lifespan development from conception to death. Identify the verses in the Qur'ān related to embryology. Describe the psychological phenomenon of cognitive, emotional and social influence on human behaviour. Discuss the role of emotion and motivation in the development of human behaviour. Discuss the nature and nature controversy in the development of intelligence. Outline one theory of motivation or spiritual from an Islāmic perspective. Discuss the issues and the dilemmas of Muslim psychologists. Discuss the Islāmic perspective of the self (*Nafs, Akl, Ruh* and *Qalb*). Identify the significance of the unseen world and its influence on human behaviour. Reflect values that are the underpinnings of psychology as a discipline. Appreciate and apply Riphah's values in the personal and professional life. Develop the capacity to reflect on and evaluate own values and priorities.

12. **Assessment**	Assessment Activity	Formative/ Summative	Weight
	Study questions	F	0
	Course portfolio and reflective practices	F	0
	Quiz, tests (MCQ tests) Sessional marks	S	30%
	Mid-term examination	F	30%
	Final examination	S	40%
	Total		100%

Introduction To Psychology

13. Prescribed Textbooks, Readings and Reference Materials	• Giorgi, A. (2020). *Psychology as a human science: A phenomenologically based approach.* Kindle Edition: University Professors Press Rassool, H, G. (2021). *Islāmic Psychology: Human Behavior and Experience from an Islāmic Perspective.* Oxford: Routledge. • University of Minnesota. (2015). *Introduction to psychology (chapter 6).* University of Minnesota's library publishing. Retrieved from https://open.lib.umn.edu/intropsyc/ • Utz, A. (2011). *Psychology from the Islāmic Perspective.* Riyadh: International Islāmic Publication House. **Key Journals** *Journal of Psychology* *British Journal of Psychology* *The American Journal of Psychology* *International Journal of Islāmic Psychology* *International Journal of Psychology*

	Curriculum Contents
Introduction	Definition of psychology. Sources of knowledge. Relationship between psychology and religion. What is Islāmic psychology? Differences between secular and Islāmic approaches to psychology. Monotheism as the basis of Islāmic psychology. Thinking critically with psychological science.
Contemporary Perspectives in Psychology	Contemporary theories of psychology. Critique of contemporary theories. Psychology versus psychiatry. Approaches to Islāmic psychology. Various school and fields of psychology. Enduring issues in psychology. Dilemmas of Muslim psychologists.
Basics of Human Nature	What is nature in psychology? Aspects of human nature. Philosophical perspective of human nature. Human nature from a secular perspective. Nature and nurture. Purpose of life story of Adam and Hawa. *Al-fitrah.* Covenant of monotheism. Good and evil. Free will and accountability. Free will and *Qadar.*
Basics of Human Nature	Definition of the soul. Nature of the soul. Connection between the self and the soul. *Qalb, Nafs, Aql and Ruh.* Stages of the *Nafs.* Weaknesses of the soul. Heart (*Qalb*) in Islāmic theory. Intention and the heart. Signs of healthy, sick and diseased heart. Poisons of the heart. Effects of sins upon the heart.
Biological Basis of Behaviour	Biological psychology. Structure and function of the neuron. Neurotransmitters and their functions. Central nervous system. Peripheral nervous system. Endocrine system. Relationship between biology and psychology.
Biological Foundation, Development and Reproductive Behaviours	Genes, chromosomes and gender determination. Dominant and recessive genes. Process of conception and prenatal development. Verses of the Qur'ān related to embryology. Pregnancy and childbirth. Potential problems associated with pregnancy.

(Continued)

	Curriculum Contents
Life Span Development: From Conception to Death	Three developmental domains. Continuity and discontinuity approaches to development. Attachment and maternal deprivation reassessed. Role of attachment in the development of parent-child relationship. Relationship between breastfeeding and bonding. Islāmic perspective on breastfeeding. issues related to marriage in Islām. Physical, cognitive and social changes that accompany late adulthood. Ageing and dying from an Islāmic perspective.
Personality	Defining personality. Definition of personality. Nature versus nurture. Secular theories of personality. Behaviourism. Humanism. Trait theory. Islāmic personality theory. Moral behaviour. Example of the Prophet (PBUH). Personality of the believers, disbelievers and hypocrites. Personality assessment.
Motivation	Definition of motivation. Need, drive and incentive. Intrinsic motivation from an Islāmic perspective. Spiritual motivation. Physiological and psychological needs and drives. Maslow's hierarchy of needs. Critique of Maslow's hierarchy of needs. Theory of motivation from an Islāmic perspective.
Emotion	Concept of emotion. Biological basis of emotion. Theories of emotion. Concept of love from an Islāmic perspective. Emotional intelligence. Emotional abilities that comprise emotional intelligence. Emotional intelligence from an Islāmic perspective. Emotional behaviours as portrayed in the Qur'ān.
Reason, Wisdom and Intelligence	Reason in psychology and Islāmic psychology. Meaning of *Aql* in the Qur'ān and from the scholars. Wisdom in psychology and Islāmic psychology. Advice Luqman gave to his son. Intelligence: theories and assessment. Nature versus nurture. Categories of intelligence.
Learning, Conditioning and Modelling	Definition of learning and conditioning. Learned behaviours, instincts and reflexes. Classical conditioning. Operant conditioning. Limitations of the behavioural approach to human learning. Observational learning. Modelling process. Contemporary learning theories from an Islāmic perspective. Spiritual modelling. Stages of observational spiritual modelling.
Memory	Definition of memory. Process of memory. Types of memory. Factors that affect memory. Types of forgetting. Strategies to improve memory. Factors involved in remembering and forgetting. Memorisation of the Qur'ān.
Social Thinking and Social Influence	Social cognition. Concepts of (1) salience and (2) priming. Social and religious cognition. Cognitive dissonance among Muslims. Attitude, prejudice, stereotypes and discrimination. Social facilitation. Theories. Conformity. Obedience. Helping behaviour.
Cognition and Language	Concept of cognition. Problem-solving, judgment and decision-making. Language development. Language and cognition. Language and culture.
State of Consciousness, Sleep and Dreaming	Define consciousness. Philosophers' and psychologists' views on consciousness. Psychology and neuroscience and consciousness. Altered state of consciousness. Unseen influences upon humans. Knowledge of the unseen with Allāh. Influence of Allāh (influence on heart/guidance, sending tranquillity, inspiration). Stages of sleep. Sleep deprivation. Islāmic perspectives on sleep etiquette.

Course Scheme

Health Psychology

1.	**Course Title**	Health Psychology
2.	**Code**	xxxx
3.	**Programme**	Bachelor of Science Degree in Psychology – BS
4.	**Department**	Psychology
5.	**Course Credits**	3
6.	**Year of Study**	2
7.	**Semester**	4
8.	**Duration**	16 weeks
9.	**Module Context**	X Core Elective
10.	**Description, Purpose and Aim(s)**	**Description** Health psychology is a specialty area that focuses on how biology, psychology, behaviour and social factors influence health and illness. The focus of the course is on an overview of the major topics, current issues and evidence-based practice surrounding the key topics in the field of health psychology. **Purpose and Aims:** The aims of the course are to develop an understanding of basic terminology, avenues of research and theoretical models in health psychology and understanding of the application of principles of health psychology in disease prevention, promoting health behaviours and health enhancement.
11.	**Intended Learning Outcomes**	Upon completion of this, students should be able to: Describe the concept health psychology and apply principles of health psychology to the understanding of disease and health behaviours. Discuss the principles underpinning health psychology theory and practice. Critically evaluate some of the models of approach in health psychology. Outline Rassool's Islāmic model of health psychology. Discuss the relationship within mind-body interactions. Identify the health beliefs systems of Muslims towards wellness and ill-health. Describe how psychosocial factors, such as stress, coping and social support, influence health behaviour and health outcomes. Identify the kinds of anxieties and stress from an Islāmic perspective. Discuss the role of exercise and physical activity for positive health outcomes. Discuss some of the problems associated with addictive behaviours. Discuss the Islāmic perspective on addictive behaviours. Outline the different models and approaches to disability. Discuss aspects of diversity and special needs according to an Islāmic perspective.

(Continued)

	Health Psychology
	Critically examine the responses or reactions to chronic conditions.
	Identify women's health issues and the interventions from secular and Islāmic perspectives.
	Discuss the stages of grief reactions according to Kubler-Ross.
	Discuss how Islām deals with the issues relation to grief and bereavement.
	Reflect Islāmic values that are the underpinnings of health psychology as a discipline in therapeutic interventions with chronically ill patients.
	Appreciate and apply Riphah's values in the caring and management of chronic illness patients.
	Embrace Riphah's values that will contribute to positive outcomes in work settings.
	Relaying hope and optimism when working with patients of chronic health illness.
	Develop the capacity to reflect on and evaluate own values and priorities.
	Have the self-awareness to commit to their own ongoing personal and professional development.

12. Assessment

Assessment Activity	Formative/ Summative	Weight
Study questions	F	0
Course portfolio and reflective practices	F	0
Quiz, tests (MCQ tests) Sessional marks	S	30%
Mid-term examination	F	30%
Final examination	S	40%
Total		100%

13. Prescribed Textbooks, Readings and Reference Materials

Gurung, R.A. (2018). *Health psychology*. Cambridge: Cambridge University Press.
Ogden, J. (2019). *Health Psychology*, 6th ed. New York: McGraw Hill.
Rassool G. Hussein. (2020). *Health and Psychology: An Islāmic Perspective*. Volume 1. London: Islāmic Psychology Publication (IIP). Amazon/Kindle.
Rassool G.Hussein. (2020). *Health and Psychology: An Islāmic Perspective*. Volume 2. London: Islāmic Psychology Publication (IIP). Amazon/Kindle.

Key Journals
Journal of Health Psychology
Health Psychology
British Journal of Health Psychology
Journal of Applied Psychology

Curriculum Contents

Introduction to Health Psychology	Definition, development and scope of health psychology. Understanding of the modern concept of health and illness. Concept of Islāmic health psychology. Difference between health psychology and Islāmic health psychology. Understanding of health psychology in Islāmic perspective.
A Framework for Attaining, Preserving and Maintaining Health	Islāmic medicine. Prophetic medicine. A framework for health psychology (Islāmic) based on the *Tawhîd* paradigm. Model of Islāmic health psychology. Models of health psychology. Health behaviours. Bio-psychosocial model.
Models and Approaches to Health Psychology	Bio-psychosocial spiritual model. The health belief model. Theory of planned behaviour/reasoned action. Transtheoretical models/theories of behaviour change. Psychoneuroimmunology model (PNI). Limitations of the models.
Health and the Individual	Distinction between psychological and physiological disorders. Health beliefs, locus of control and self-efficacy. Psychosocial health. Mind-body interactions. Psychosomatic medicine. Psychological factors in illness. Religious belief and health. Personality type and health. Locus of control.
Health Beliefs and the Muslim	Health beliefs. Islām and Culture. Health & Illness. Understanding the Muslim patient's view of illness and disease. Medical consultation and examination. Beliefs affecting health interventions.
Stress, Coping and Health	What is stress? Stress and the endocrine system. Theories of stress. Symptoms of stress. Psychoneuroimmunology. Kinds of anxieties. Islāmic perspectives (Sheikh Muhammed Salih Al-Munajjid). How can we measure stress? Coping strategies. Stress management. Islāmic perspectives on coping with stress.
Lifestyles and Health	Nutrition risk factors. Reduce your risk of illness. Weight and health. Obesity and overweight and their causes. Health consequences of obesity. Islāmic guidance on food and health. Approved and forbidden food. Reduction of obesity from an Islāmic perspective.
Physical Activity and Sport	Physical activity and exercise. Benefits of exercise. Physical activity and exercise from an Islāmic perspective. Barriers facing Muslim women's participation in exercise.
Addictive Behaviours and Society: An Islāmic Perspective	Concept of addiction and addictive behaviour. Relationship between addiction and society. Tolerance, physical dependence psychological dependence and craving. Characteristics of addictive behaviours. Theories of addiction. Stages of addiction. Research involving spirituality and addiction.
Chronic Illnesses: Coping and Rehabilitation	Concept of chronic illness. Responses or reactions to chronic conditions. Relationship with others or with carers. Approaches people use in dealing with uncertainty. Islāmic perspective in response to chronic illness
Women's Health Issues	Concept of family planning. Permanent and temporary methods of contraception. Family planning from an Islāmic perspective. Problems associated with infertility. Halal approach in the treatment of infertility. Abortion: scientific, legal and moral perspectives.

(Continued)

114 Course scheme in Islāmic psychology

Curriculum Contents

Grief and Bereavement	Basic reactions to death (Kubler-Ross). Symptoms and stages of grief. Beliefs people hold towards death and dying from around the world. Children's views on death and how they cope with grieving. Acceptance, adjustment and coping with chronic and terminal illnesses. Working with the individual/community. Euthanasia from an Islāmic perspective. Death and dying from an Islāmic perspective.
Health Promotion and Behaviour Change	Concept of health promotion. Health promotion activities from an Islāmic perspective. Islāmic charter for health promotion. Models of health promotion. Health promotion programs for public awareness and disease prevention. Effectiveness of health promotion.
Research in Health Psychology	Research in health psychology. Qualitative data collection. Interviews and focus groups. Discourse and narrative analysis. Questionnaires and surveys. Intervention studies. Bio-ethics and health psychology. Systematic reviews, meta-analyses and preference analyses.

Course Scheme

History and Perspectives in Psychology

1. **Course Title**: History and Perspectives in Psychology
2. **Code**: xxxx
3. **Programme**: Bachelor of Science Degree in Psychology – BS
4. **Department**: Psychology
5. **Course Credits**: 3
6. **Year of Study**: 1
7. **Semester**: 1
8. **Duration**: 16 weeks
9. **Module Context**: X   Core   Elective
10. **Description, Purpose and Aim(s)**:
    Description:
    The course is about the evolution of history and psychology from a Eurocentric and Islāmic perspectives and the different schools of psychology thoughts.

    Purpose and Aims:
    This course aims to examine the development of classical, modern Western psychology and Islāmic psychology. It also explores the different schools of psychology thought and perspectives. The course will also focus both classical and contemporary scholars who influenced the beginnings and development of Islāmic psychology.
11. **Intended Learning Outcomes**: Upon completion of this, students should be able to:
    Identify the relationship between philosophy, physiology and psychology.
    Outline a brief history in the development of psychology from a Judeo-Christian perspective.
    Explain the following terms: structuralism, functionalism, constructivism, realism.
    Discuss the factors in the rise and decline of the Islāmic Golden Age.
    Examine the contributions of the different schools of psychology in the understanding human behaviours and experiences.

		History and Perspectives in Psychology		
		Discuss the limitations and strengths of the different schools of psychology. Examine the relationship between the Qur'ān and human behaviour. Describe the contributions of classical Islāmic philosophers to the development of Islāmic psychology. Describe the contributions of classical Islāmic physicians to the development of Islāmic psychology. Describe the contributions of classical Islāmic theologians to the development of Islāmic psychology. Critically examine the work of contemporary Islāmic psychologist in the Islāmisation of psychology. Discuss the contributions of contemporary thinkers and scholars and clinicians in the development of Islāmic psychology. Discuss the issues for Muslim psychologists in Badri's *The Dilemma of Muslim Psychologists*. Critically examine the work of contemporary Islāmic psychologists in the Islāmisation of psychology. Discuss the relative merits of the Islāmisation of knowledge in the decolonising of psychology. Appreciate and apply Riphah's values in Islāmic psychology. Develop the capacity to reflect and be critical in the different narratives of psychology.		
12.	**Assessment**	*Assessment Activity*	*Formative/ Summative*	*Weight*
		Study questions	F	0
		Course portfolio and reflective practices	F	0
		Quiz, tests (MCQ tests) Sessional marks	S	30%
		Mid-term examination	F	30%
		Final examination	S	40%
		Total		100%
13.	**Prescribed Textbooks, Readings and Reference Materials**	Haque, A. (2004). Psychology from Islāmic Perspective: Contributions of Early Muslim Scholars and Challenges to Contemporary Muslim Psychologists. *Journal of Religion and Health*, 43(4), 357–377. Hothersall, D., & Lovett, B.J. (2022). *History of psychology*. Cambridge: Cambridge University Press. Rassool, G. Hussein, & Luqman, M. (2022). *Foundations of Islāmic Psychology: From Classical Scholars to Contemporary Thinkers*. Oxford: Routledge. Wertheimer, M., & Puente, A.E. (2020). *A brief history of psychology*. Oxford: Routledge. **Key Journals** *History of Psychology* **History and Philosophy of Psychology** *European Yearbook of the History of Psychology* *International Journal of Islāmic Psychology*		

(Continued)

116 Course scheme in Islāmic psychology

Curriculum Contents	
Introduction to the History and Philosophy of Psychology	History and perspectives in psychology. Brief history of psychology. Philosophy and physiology contributions to the development of psychology. Psychology emerges as a separate discipline. Major approaches of *Kalam* (understanding the nature of things). Development and decline of the Islāmic Golden Age. The birth of Islāmic psychology.
Schools of Psychology	Aristotle (384–322 BC). Rene Descartes (1596–1650). John Locke (1632–1704). Charles Darwin (1809–1882). Francis Galton (1822–1911). William James. Wilhelm Wundt (1832–1920). Structuralism: psychology's first school of thought. Edward B. Titchener. The functionalism of William James. Constructivism. Realism. The emergence of psychoanalysis. The rise of behaviourism. John. B. Watson. The third force in psychology.
Schools of Psychology	Existential perspective; Thomas Szaz and Victor Frankel. Gestalt perspective: Fritz Perls. Humanistic perspective: Carl Rogers and Abraham Maslow. Cognitive psychology. Positive psychology. Women in psychology history: Mary Whiton Calkins, Anna Freud and Mary Ainsworth.
Evolution and Development of Islāmic Psychology	Introduction to the history and philosophy of psychology: an Islāmic perspective. The Golden Age of Islām. The rise and decline of the Golden Age of Islām. Mutazilites and Ash'arite movement. Problems with Muslim philosophers. The Qur'ān, Sunnah and Islāmic psychology. Philosophers, physicians and theologians.
Classical Scholars: Philosophers	Abu Yusuf Yaqub Ibn Ishaq Al-Kindi: the Great Arab Philosopher. Importance and value of divine virtues. Contributions to Islāmic scholarship. Reconciling Muslim faith with Greek philosophy. Contributions of Al-Kindi to philosophy and psychology.
Classical Scholars: Philosophers	Abu Ali Ahmad b. Muhammad b. Ya'kub Ibn Miskawayh. Abu'al Walid Muhammad ibn Ahmad ibn Muhammad Ibn Rushd.
Classical Scholars: Physicians	Abdu Bakr Mohamed Ibn Zakariya Al-Rāzī. Abu Ali al-Husayn Ibn Abdullah Ibn Sīnā. Their lives, books on psychology, their views on psychology and therapeutic interventions (if appropriate).
Classical Scholars: Physicians	Abu Zayd Ahmed ibn Sahl al-Balkhī. Al-Balkhi's book on psychology. Mind-body connection. Psychology and psychopathology. Depressive disorders. Phobias. Obsessive-compulsive disorder. Therapeutic interventions.
Classical Scholars: Theologians	Abu Hamid Muhammad al-Ghazālī. Sunni Ash'arite theology. Al-Ghazālī: Sufism. Al-Ghazālī: his works. Al-Ghazālī: concept of self. Al-Ghazālī: disciplining the soul. Al-Ghazālī: religious law (*Shar'iah*). The concept of children education in Islām. Curriculum. Principles: methods of teaching and techniques. Psychological studies through Islāmic guidance. Spiritual psychology. Psychopathology. Therapeutic interventions and self-purification.

Curriculum Contents

Classical Scholars: Theologians	Ibn Taymiyyah al-Ḥarrānī. Disease of their heart and cure. Understanding of the *Nafs*. *Aql* and *Ishq*. Conditions of the heart. Ibn Qayyim al Jawziyyah. Methodology of understanding psycho-spiritual diseases and their cure. Psychosomatic concept. Curing psychological and spiritual illnesses. Psychological treatment. Changing thinking process.
Classical Scholars: Theologians	Al-Raghib Ar-Rāghib al-Aṣbahānī. Jamāl al-Dīn Abū al-Faraj 'Abd al-Raḥmān Ibn al-Jawzī. Ibn Khaldūn al-Ḥaḍramī... Ibn Rajab al-Hanbali. Contributions to the understanding of Islāmic psychology.
Scholars, Academics and Clinicians	Allama Muhammad Iqbal (Pakistan). Levels of self-development. Allama Iqbal on psychology. Iqbal's theory of personality. Some aspects of the ego. Iqbal's concept on ego/*Khudi*/self. Personality according to *Iqbal*. Elements that weaken the personality. Stages of personality development. Ideal society for personality development. Sayyid Abul A'la Maududi (India/Pakistan). Ideology of Abul Ala Maududi. The ideology of Abul A'la Maududi. Syed Muhammad Al Naquib Bin Ali Al-Attas. International Institute of Islāmic Thought and Civilisation. Islāmisation of knowledge: behavioural sciences. Bio-information: Isma'il Raji Al-Faruqi. Isma'il Raji Al-Faruqi: books. Islāmisation. Professor Ibrahim A. Ragab. A methodology for Islāmisation of knowledge. Islāmisation process: the engagement approach. Islāmisation process: the disengagement approach. Islāmisation process: the correct approach. Dealing with psychosocial problems: Islāmic perspectives. Islāmisation of knowledge in the behavioural sciences. Approach for a methodology for Islāmisation of knowledge. Psychosocial problems from an Islāmic perspective.
Scholars, Academics and Clinicians	Malik Badri, his contributions to the revival of Islāmic psychology (Sudan). The father of modern Islāmic psychology.
Scholars, Academics and Clinicians	Life, works, contributions and views on Islāmic psychology: Amber Haque (US/India). Rasjid Skinner (UK). Akhbar Husain (India). Rania Awaad (US/Egypt). Muhammad Tahir Khalily (Pakistan).
Scholars, Academics and Clinicians	Life, works, contributions and views on Islāmic psychology: Suleyman Derin (Turkey). Hamid Rafiei Honar (Iran). Saleh bin Ibrahim Al-Sanie (Saudi Arabia). Ola Pavlova (Russia).
Scholars, Academics and Clinicians	Life, works, contributions, and views of Islāmic psychology: G. Hussein Rassool (UK/Mauritius).

Course Scheme

Social Psychology

1.	Course Title	Social Psychology
2.	Code	xxxx
3.	Programme	Bachelor of Science Degree in Psychology – BS
4.	Department	Psychology
5.	Course Credits	3
6.	Year of Study	2
7.	Semester	3
8.	Duration	16 weeks
9.	Module Context	X Core Elective
10.	Description, Purpose and Aim(s)	**Description:** The course emphasises on the understanding of application of social psychology concepts in the real-life settings with reference to Islāmic and Western perspectives. **Purpose and Aims:** The aims of the course are to examine the theories and conceptual framework of social psychology and how they can explain social behaviour from both secular and Islāmic perspectives. The course will also enable students to think critically about social processes, influences, relations and attitudes.
11.	Intended Learning Outcomes	Upon completion of this, students should be able to: Define social psychology. Discuss the role of social perception in the understanding of social behaviour. Outline the self in a social world. Discuss the role of emotion and motivation in the understanding of social behaviour. Critically examine the functions of prosocial behaviours in contemporary society. Evaluate the significance of Milgram's obedience study in understanding human behaviour. Describe the differences between individualistic and collectivist cultures approach to relationships. Evaluate how the Hawthorn studies contribute to our understanding of group influences. Discuss how Fishbein's multi-attribute theory can explain consumer behaviour. Identify three factors that can facilitate attraction and three that can cause prejudice. Compare and contrast the social learning and biological perspectives of aggression. List the reasons that people conform. Discuss the Islāmic perspective on prejudice. Describe the stages in the theory of reasoned action according to Fishbein.

		Social Psychology		
		Evaluate how cognitive dissonance can influence human behaviour. Discuss how the person and situation can interact to improve motivation. Explain three ways mental effort can be conserved through a process of social cognition. Demonstrate awareness of cultural differences in collectivist and individualistic cultures. Outline the contribution of Al-Fārābī to social psychology. Outline the work of Ibn Khaldun to educational sociology.		
12.	Assessment	Assessment Activity	Formative/ Summative	Weight
		Study questions	F	0
		Course portfolio and reflective practices	F	0
		Quiz, tests (MCQ tests) Sessional marks	S	30%
		Mid-term examination	F	30%
		Final examination	S	40%
		Total		100%
13.	Prescribed Textbooks, Readings and Reference Materials	Rassool, G. Hussein. (2021). *Islāmic Psychology: Human Behavior and Experience from an Islāmic Perspective.* Oxford: Routledge. Myers, D.G. (2012). *Social psychology* (11th ed.). New York: McGraw-Hill. University of Minnesota (2015). *Principles in Social Psychology.* University of Minnesota's library publishing. https://open.lib.umn.edu/socialpsychology. **Key Journals** *The Journal of Social Psychology* *Journal of Personality and Social Psychology* *Journal of Applied Social Psychology* *International Journal of Islāmic Psychology*		

	Curriculum Contents
Social Psychology	What is social psychology? The components of social psychology. Social psychology and allied disciplines. Brief history of social psychology. Current trends in social psychology. Al-Farabi's social psychology. Ibn Khaldun's theory of social psychology.
Social Perception	Components of social perception: observation, attribution, integration and confirmation. Attribution theories. Impressions. Information integration theory. Accuracy of social perception. Factors influencing social perception. Examples of social perception. Social cognition, person schemas, roles and scripts. Impression formation. Stereotypes. Attribution. Bias in attribution. Research on attribution.

(Continued)

Curriculum Contents

Self in a Social World	Social self. The role of the social situation. Components of self: why they are essential and its relationship to other personality constructs and processes. Looking-glass self. Labelling bias, self-labelling and internalised prejudice. Social comparison. Social identity. Self-evaluation maintenance theory. The self from an Islāmic perspective. Discovering the self in Islām: self-striving, self-regard and self-neglect. Self-presentation.
Emotion	Concept of emotion. Biological and neurological bases of emotion. Theories of emotion. Culture and expressions of emotions. Emotional intelligence. An Islāmic perspective. The Qur'ān and emotional behaviour.
Prosocial Behaviour: Altruism	Altruism. Why does it exist? Evolution/biological reasons. Sociocultural reasons. Neurocognitive reasons. Altruism from an Islāmic perspective. Degree of altruism.
Prosocial Behaviour: Helping	Helping behaviours. Types of helping behaviours. Helping behaviour from an Islāmic perspective. Positive and negative moods on helping behaviours. Latane and Darley's decision model of helping.
Aggression	Aggression. Psychological perspectives on aggression: psychoanalytic, biological, behavioural, cognitive. The motivation to harm. Islāmic perspective on aggression: other views. Frustration and aggression. Threatened self-esteem and aggression. Controlling and socialising for non-aggressive ways of conflict resolution.
Theories of Relationships	Why do we form relationships? Biological theories of relationships. Matching hypothesis. Social exchange theory. Cultural aspects of relationships Individualistic versus collectivist cultures. Parental influence. Peer influence. Factors that lead to and promote attraction. Need for affiliation. Theories of love.
Behaviour and Attitudes	Attitude formation. Prejudice, stereotypes and discrimination. What does Islām say about prejudice? Prejudice and discrimination. Islāmic views on prejudice. Characteristics of prejudice in Islām. Consequences of prejudice. Attitude change. Cognitive dissonance. Persuasive communication. Measurement of attitudes. Application of social psychological principles for *Tarbiyah* and *Da'wah* in organisation. The Islāmic perspective on social work.
Social Influence and Group Behaviour	Nature of groups. Group polarisation. Teamwork in Islām. De-individuation, group cohesiveness, productivity and decision-making. Conformity, obedience and deviance, and cultural and social norms. Effective leadership. Concept of leadership. Quality of a good leader in Islām. Theories of leadership.
Islāmic Perspectives on Social Psychology	Examples from the Qur'ān and Ḥādīth. Acceptable and non-acceptable aspects of social behaviour. Social cognition: impression formation. Attitude: prejudice and discrimination. Social influence: compliance.
Conformity and Obedience	Conformity. Types of social influence. Cognitive dissonance. Bystander effect. Obedience. Milgram's experiment. Variants of Milgram's experiment. Why do people obey? Personality theories. Legitimate authority. Agency theory. Compliance techniques. Presence of allies. Why don't people obey?
People in Groups: Foundations of Group Behaviour	People in groups. Foundations of group behaviour. Types of groups. Why do people join groups? Group influence. How do minorities influence? Conditions required for minority influence to be successful. Conversion theory. Social impact theory. Social identity theory.

Course scheme in Islāmic psychology 121

Curriculum Contents

Motivation	What is motivation? Extrinsic and intrinsic motivation. Instinct theory of motivation. The drive-reduction theory. Incentive theory of motivation. Humanistic theory of motivation. Muslim's scholars' perception of Maslow's model. Spirituality and motivation. Spiritual model of motivation. Islāmic models of motivation.
Al-Fārābī Social Psychology	The virtuous city (*Madina Fadylya*). Social psychology and principles of the opinions of the citizens of the virtuous city. Perfect society: the great, medium and small. Virtue, the best moral quality. Three types depending on the judgment and temperament. Non-virtuous city: three types (ignorant city, wicked city, misguided city). Necessary city, city exchange, city meanness, city of ambition, power-hungry city, voluptuous city. Imam – the head of the virtuous city. Understanding of man as a spiritual and bodily unity. Virtuous people and a model of the perfect man.
Ibn Khaldun's Sociology	The founding father of sociology. Concept of education in the *Muqaddima*. Education – the replication of individuals and groups, firstly at the level of values and secondly at that of knowledge and know-how. The education system in Muslim societies. The reproduction of values. Training in knowledge and know-how. Learning the arts. The teaching of the sciences. Conditions for teaching. Pedagogical principles. Methods and contents.

Course Scheme

Biological Basis of Behaviour

1.	Course Title	Biological Basis of Behaviour		
2.	Code	xxxx		
3.	Programme	Bachelor of Science Degree in Psychology – BS		
4.	Department	Psychology		
5.	Course Credits	3		
6.	Year of Study	2		
7.	Semester	3		
8.	Duration	16 weeks		
9.	Module Context	X	Core	Elective
10.	Description, Purpose and Aim(s)	Description: This course will introduce the basic concepts of the physiological and neurobiological mechanisms underlying the generation and control of behaviour. Purpose and Aims: The aims are to understand the mechanisms of input-process-output of the brain and the mechanisms through which the five senses are perceived in the brain. In addition, the focus is on linking between biological and psychological factors underlying human behaviour and disorders.		
11.	Intended Learning Outcomes	Upon completion of this, students should be able to: Describe the basic brain and nervous system anatomy and functions. Identify the techniques used in biopsychology and neuroscience. Differentiate between Islāmic and Western perspectives of biological basis of behaviour.		

(*Continued*)

		Biological Basis of Behaviour		
		Explain why biological basis of behaviour is useful for a Muslim psychologist. Describe the biological basis of vision. Describe how the flow of information works in sensation and action. Explain the basic methods of psychophysics of perception. Recognise how the brain mechanisms mediate planning and motivation. Describe the problems associated with memory disorders. Discuss learning and memorisation from an Islāmic perspective. Describe the stages of the embryo based on the Qur'ān. Describe the role of hormones in biopsychology. Discuss the specific challenges for eating disorders. Outline the neural basis of sleep. Critically examine the biological perspective on mental health Discuss the role of neurochemical transmitters in the understanding of mood disorders. Outline the neuroscience of motivation. Identify some of the neurological disorders and their possible causes. Identify some of the neuroimaging techniques in assessment of neurological disorders.		
12.	Assessment	*Assessment Activity*	*Formative/ Summative*	*Weight*
		Study questions	F	0
		Course portfolio and reflective practices	F	0
		Quiz, tests (MCQ tests) Sessional marks	S	30%
		Mid-term examination	F	30%
		Final examination	S	40%
		Total		100%
13.	**Prescribed Textbooks, Readings and Reference Materials**	Carlson, N.R. (2015). *Foundation of physiological psychology* (6th ed.). Boston: Allyn and Bacon. D'Amato, R.C., Davis, A.S., Power, E.M., & Eusebio, E.C. (2021). *Understanding the Biological Basis of Behavior: Developing Evidence-Based Interventions for Clinical, Counseling and School Psychologists*. Switzerland: Springer Nature. Khan, M.A., & Aftab, A. (2020). *Quran-i-Hakeem and Embryology*. Lahore: Idara Matboot-i-Sulemani. Pinel, J.P. (2016). *Biopsychology* (6th ed.). UK: Allyn and Bacon. Rassool, G. Hussein. (2021). *Islāmic Psychology: Human Behavior and Experience from an Islāmic Perspective*. Oxford: Routledge. **Key Journals** *Behavioral Biology* *Biopsychology* *The Journal of Biological Psychology*		

Course scheme in Islāmic psychology 123

Curriculum Contents

Introduction to Biological Bases of Behaviour	Introduction to neuropsychology and related terminology. Differences in Islāmic and Western perspectives on biological bases of behaviour. History of the discipline. Current trends in the field of behavioural neuroscience. Contribution of various areas and related disciplines
Islāmic Biological Psychology	History of neurosciences and biological bases of behaviour. Islāmic terminology related to the brain and neuroscience. Islāmic history and contributions to biological psychology.
Structure and Function of Nervous System	Neurons and glial cells. The neuron: neuronal characteristics, types, transmission and communication systems. Neuroanatomical directional terms and planes of reference. Structures of nervous system and their functions and connections
The Central Nervous System	Forebrain, midbrain, hindbrain. Spinal cord. Peripheral nervous system. Autonomic nervous system. Different functional regions in the brain; brain anatomy. The first evidence of localisation. Maps of brain function. Neuroimaging studies. The brain and affective states. Mental processing.
Research Methods	Scientific methods of research – basic research. Electroencephalography; neuroimaging. Clinical research – lesions, split-brain studies, genetic studies.
Methods of Studying the Nervous System	Glands. Endocrine glands. Types of glands. Function of glands. Effect of hormones on human behaviour. Neurochemistry. Characteristics of neurotransmitters, neuromodulators and neurohormones. Major neurotransmitters: dopamine, norepinephrine, serotonin, acetylcholine, GABA, glycine, peptides (opiates).
The Senses: Touch and Vision	Touch – sub-modalities, development of touch. Vision – history of vision science. Gestalt psychology and visual processing. Equilibrium, hearing, smell, taste. Senses and receptors. Qur'ānic perspective.
The Senses: Hearing, Smell and Taste	Touch and vision summary. Hearing – the ear, hearing aids, hearing range, hearing in the brain, sounds localisation. Equilibrium – the vestibular system, vertigo. Smell – the path of olfaction. How smells are distinguished. Taste – taste buds, detection of tastes. Qur'ānic perspective.
Perception and Sensation	What is perception? Sensation and perception. Perceptual representation and systems of perception. Sensation – the travel of sensation. Difference between the senses. Somatosensory and touch. Pain, vision, equilibrium, hearing, smell, taste. Perceptual disorders.
Learning and Memory	Neuroscience of learning. Psychology of learning. Forms of learning – habituation, memorisation. Rewards and learning – classical conditioning. Learning and memorisation from an Islāmic perspective.
Memory and Amnesia	Memory and amnesia. Involvement of brain in memory. Memory disorders (Korsakov, Alzheimer's, Parkinson's diseases, among others).
Motivation	Homeostasis. Involvement of brain and neurotransmitters in motivational behaviour. The pyramid of needs (Maslow). Needs of survival versus wanting. Neuroscience of motivation. The neurobiology of volition. Planning and judgement. Psychological assessment of planning. An Islāmic perspective on needs and motivation.

(Continued)

	Curriculum Contents
Embryology from the Qur'ān	Basic facts about reproduction. Qur'ānic versions about human procreation. Creation of Adam. Concept of two sexes. Procreation. Development stages of embryo. Other topics of reproduction. Old age as a causal factor of sterility. Semen and its constituents. Overview of the practical implications of human reproduction as revealed in the Qur'ān.
Behavioural Disorders	Taste perception – recap of taste sense. Eating disorders – definition, types and classification, therapy for eating disorders. Cognitive behavioural therapy and eating disorders. Islāmic perception and Islāmic therapy for eating disorders. Specific challenges in eating disorders. Ramadan and Islāmic guidelines for eating.
Neurological Disorders	Variability of symptoms. Psychiatric versus neurologic disorders. Brain injury, brain tumour, neurodegenerative diseases, mental disorders. The diagnostic process. Clinical cases: epilepsy, cerebral palsy, multiple sclerosis. Psychiatric disorders with organic/biochemical aetiology: mood disorder, anxiety disorders, schizophrenia, mental retardation.
Sleep	Definitions and discussion of sleep. Sleep and its relationship to health. The stages of sleep. The brain during sleep. Sleep disorders. Sleep disturbance as an index of psychological problems. Sleep guidelines in Islām.

Bibliography

Oxford Reference. (2022). www.oxfordreference.com/view/10.1093/oi/authority.20110803100445418 (accessed 7 October 2022).

Index

abnormal 15, 84, 104
abortion 113
AbuSulayman 37, 42, 44, 85
accountability 48, 76, 109
acculturation 18
acetylcholine 123
acquisition 3, 23, 25, 28, 31, 32, 47, 51, 95
actualise 31
adab 25, 27, 31
adaptation 67, 68, 81, 87
addiction 66, 113
addictive 111, 113
adoption 6, 37, 66, 77, 95
adults 25, 81, 82
advocates 29
aetiology 124
affecting 27, 82, 100, 113
affiliation 120
afterlife 8
ageing 110
agenda-setting 76
aggression 118, 120
Ahlus-Sunnah 9
Al-Attas 25, 26, 30–32, 34, 35, 37, 38, 44, 45
Akhirah-oriented 48, 76
akhlāq 8, 67, 76
Akl 108
al-amanah 101
al-Balkhī 116
alcohol 41, 66, 83
Al-Fārābī 26, 28, 29, 31, 34, 119, 121
Al-Farūqī 26, 29–31, 34, 37, 38, 40, 101
Al-Ghazālî 25–29, 31, 33, 34
al-īmān 9
al-Islām 8

Al-Kindi 116
Allāh 4, 6, 9, 11, 110
al-Nafs 31
alternative 38, 42, 50, 89
altruism 120
Alzheimer's 123
amalgam 90, 99
analogous 29
anathema 17, 37
animistic 38
anthropology 9, 33, 89
anti-Islāmic 17
antithesis 36
anxieties 66, 111, 113
aqli 5, 62
Aristotle 116
Ar-Rāghib 117
ar-Ruboobeeyah 8
articulation 16, 55, 104, 105
Ash'arite 116
assessments 54, 57, 92
assignments 54, 57
attachment 110
at-Tirmidhi 22
attitudes 18, 23, 44, 47, 51, 53, 55, 58, 62, 66–68, 77, 80–83, 86, 92, 95, 96, 118, 120
attribution 119
audio-visual 81
autonomic 123
axiology 26, 32

Badri 11, 15, 19–21, 40, 44, 117
behavioural 29, 49, 50, 108, 110, 117, 120, 123, 124
behaviourism 110, 116
behaviours 8, 11, 12, 15, 17, 32, 49, 62, 64, 65, 68, 71–73, 77, 80, 82,

126 Index

104, 107, 109–111, 113, 114, 118, 120
beliefs 9, 11, 18, 23, 27, 32, 36, 38, 41, 65, 68, 71, 77, 81, 111, 113, 114
bereavement 112, 114
Berghout's 100, 101, 103
biases 12, 15
bibliography 19, 34, 44, 59, 81, 97, 105, 124
biochemical 124
bio-ethics 104, 114
bio-information 117
biology 109, 111, 122
biomedical 13
biopsychology 121, 122
bio-psychosocial 2, 33, 104, 113
birth 26, 116
blinded 15
blueprint 97
boundaries 24, 44, 57, 66, 88, 98
breastfeeding 110
bystander 120

caffeine 41
cardiovascular 104
caring 112
cataclysmic 41
categories 39, 40, 89, 110
causes 113, 122
challenges 14, 17–19, 43, 44, 96, 115, 122, 124
character-building 32
characterisation 54
characteristics 9, 17, 30, 51, 70, 78, 95, 96, 113, 120, 123
Charybdis 16
childbirth 109
childhood 35, 45
children 116
chromosomes 109
chronological 55
civilisation 4, 24, 38, 89, 90, 117
classical 2, 7, 16, 22, 24, 26, 28–31, 35, 36, 43, 52, 61, 64, 83, 91, 96, 104, 110, 114–117, 123
classification 3, 54, 59, 124
classroom 77, 83
climate 17, 27
clinical 1, 2, 12–14, 19, 49, 52, 54, 56, 57, 61, 67, 69, 75, 76, 84, 92, 96, 99, 122–124
clinicians 19, 94, 96, 115, 117
clones 64

closed-mindedness 10
close-ended 67
coefficient 67–69, 73
co-existence 10
cognisant 52
cognition 2, 3, 110, 119, 120
cognitive 18, 21, 26, 35, 45, 50, 51, 54, 66, 78, 82, 98, 100, 104–106, 108, 110, 116, 119, 120, 124
cohort 101
collection 21, 69, 79, 114
collectivist 118–120
colonial 11–14, 36, 37
colonisation 1, 12, 13, 36, 64
communication 45, 54, 77, 82, 86, 89, 120, 123
compartmentalised 24
competence 2, 11, 15, 23, 47, 56
complementary 7, 17, 87
compliance 120
components 54, 66, 77, 101, 103, 108, 119, 120
compulsory 27
conceptions 44, 45
concepts 2, 22, 24, 26, 31–33, 37, 40, 42, 56, 60, 65, 75, 77, 86, 92, 104, 107, 110, 118, 121
conceptualisations 6
conclusions 40, 66, 89
conditioning 11, 12, 28, 29, 110, 123
confidentiality 53, 69
conform 118
conformity 110, 120
consciousness 6, 25, 33, 36, 37, 110
consensus 29, 41, 78
consent 53, 69
constructivism 114, 116
contemplating 4
contemplation 65
contemporary 1, 6, 11, 16, 17, 21, 22, 26, 31, 34, 35, 39–44, 52, 61, 62, 64, 83, 88, 104, 109, 110, 114, 115, 118
context 2, 6, 7, 9, 10, 13–15, 18, 29, 37, 39, 42, 47, 53, 59–63, 66, 67, 84, 85, 90, 93, 95, 96, 99, 107, 111, 114, 118, 121
contraception 113
contributions 21, 37, 49, 68, 87, 114–117, 123
conversion 38, 120
coordination 87, 88, 93
cosmology 31

counselling 2, 33, 52–54, 62, 84, 96, 105
covenant 9, 109
criteria 7, 15, 67
criticisms 29, 41
Cronbach's 68
cross-cultural 13, 84
cultural 2, 11, 15, 22, 27, 30, 36, 37, 42–44, 91, 107, 119, 120
culture 14, 15, 18, 23, 24, 28, 50, 51, 66, 78, 89, 96, 97, 110, 113, 120
curriculum 1, 12–21, 23, 27, 29, 31–33, 35, 36, 43–45, 47–52, 54–68, 74–76, 79, 80, 82, 84–88, 90–101, 103–107, 109, 110, 113, 114, 116, 117, 119–121, 123, 124
curriculum-integration 98

dangers 12
Darussalam 20, 22
death 108, 110, 114
decades 10
decision-behaviour 120
decision-making 58, 110
decolonisation 2, 14, 19, 90
decolonise 1, 2, 18, 97
decolonising 1, 14, 15, 17, 19–22, 35, 45, 82, 98, 99, 106, 115
deconstruct 90
deconstruction 48, 94
deduction 8
definition 12, 34, 38, 41, 47, 60, 109, 110, 113, 124
democracy 23, 34, 44
democratic 12
demographic 67, 69, 70, 72, 76
demonstration 29, 53
depressive 116
deprivation 110
description 107, 111, 114, 118, 121
desecularisation 41, 43
design 32, 47–49, 51, 52, 54–56, 58–60, 67, 86, 87, 92, 98, 103, 105
determinism 17
developmental 10, 55, 64, 110
deviation 68–71
dhikr 3
diabetes 104
diagnostic 58, 124
dichotomy 6, 7
diffusion 18, 66
dimensions 9, 11, 26, 27, 30–33, 65, 67, 86, 89, 90, 103, 107

disbelievers 110
discipline 1, 6, 10, 16, 17, 24, 25, 28, 32, 40, 55, 61, 63, 86–88, 90, 91, 97, 99, 104, 108, 112, 116, 123
discrimination 39, 110, 120
disease 104, 111, 113, 114, 117
disengagement 66, 89, 117
disintegrating 26, 32
disorders 13, 113, 116, 121–124
disposition 67
dissemination 89, 93, 95, 100
dissociated 13
dissonance 17, 18, 99, 110, 119, 120
diversification 15, 22
diversity 1, 15, 20, 21, 32, 36, 42, 44, 47, 95, 111
dogma 11
dopamine 123
dreaming 110
drinking 83
drive-reduction 121
drug 81, 83
duality 18, 36, 43, 65
dying 110, 114
dynamism 6

eccentrics 15
economics 39, 81
education 7, 14, 15, 20, 21, 23–37, 44, 45, 48, 49, 51, 55–57, 59, 60, 66, 70, 78, 80, 81, 83, 85, 87–89, 93–95, 97, 98, 100, 101, 103–105, 116, 121
educational-development 59
educators 37, 50, 80, 92
educere 30
effectiveness 44, 58, 100, 114
ego 117
e-Learning 81
Electroencephalography 123
embedded 10, 21, 33, 35, 36, 45, 62, 63, 65, 82, 95, 98, 99, 103, 106
embryo 122, 124
embryology 108, 109, 122, 124
emergence 6, 10, 74, 97, 116
emotion 108, 110, 118, 120
emotional 2, 26, 108, 110, 120
empiricism 5, 7, 9, 10, 17
empowerment 56
encapsulate 49
Encyclopaedia 35, 44, 60
endocrine 109, 113, 123
endocrinology 104

Index

engagement 56, 89, 117
engineering 44
enhancement 111
environment 27, 49, 65
epilepsy 124
epistemological 2, 8, 9, 14, 21, 31, 39, 41–43, 62, 89, 90, 98
epistemologies 12, 14
epistemology 2, 32, 34, 43, 62, 104
ethical 8, 10, 11, 19, 23, 24, 33, 39, 41, 48, 53, 58, 61–64, 66–69, 74–80, 82, 84, 101
ethicalisation 32, 34
ethics 2, 11, 12, 14, 16–18, 26–28, 30–34, 38, 40, 44, 47, 50–53, 61–65, 67, 69, 71, 74–78, 80, 84, 89–91, 94, 99, 100, 103–105
ethnic 24
ethnicity 21
etymologically 7
Eurocentrism 23
euthanasia 114
evaluation 18, 29, 48–50, 52, 54, 56, 58–60, 80, 93, 95, 97–101, 103
evidence 1, 7, 13, 33, 48, 62, 66, 76–78, 88, 123
evidence-based 111, 122
evolution 17, 33, 37, 61, 91, 114, 116, 120
evolutionary 42, 104
exclusion 11, 16
exegesis 4, 84, 90
existential 7, 116
experiential 51, 56
experimentation 10

façade 13
facilitation 110
factors 19, 37, 40, 55, 61, 66, 77, 78, 81–83, 97, 99, 110, 111, 113, 114, 118–121
faith 8–10, 25, 27, 31–33, 116
faith-based 2
Fard-e-Ain 27
Fard-e-Kifaya 27
Farūqī 34
feedback 57, 58, 60, 92, 95, 100, 101
findings 15, 64, 69, 71, 73, 76–81, 90, 94
fissure 1
focus 10, 12, 16, 24, 48, 50, 52, 53, 58, 69, 74, 86, 94, 95, 99, 100, 111, 114, 121
foetus 104
forensic 84

formative 56–58, 92, 108, 112, 115, 119, 122
foundations 8, 49, 60, 94, 99, 115, 120
founding 121
fragmentation 10
freedom 50, 70
Freud 64, 116
function 66, 92, 95, 109, 123
functionalism 114, 116
fundamental 6, 8, 29, 35, 42, 49, 54, 67, 89, 101, 105
future 22, 58, 80, 82, 92, 94

gatekeeper 56
Genealogy 21
generalisations 79
generation 121
Gestalt 85, 116, 123
globalisation 12, 13, 36, 64
goal 19, 28, 31–33, 47, 62
goal-directed 42
God 5, 7, 8, 23–26, 28–31, 40, 76, 99–101
governmental 36
grading 57, 92
Graduate 34
graduates 1
graduating 1
grieving 114
grounded 31
guardian 7
guidance 5, 25, 28, 74, 78, 101, 110, 113, 116
guidelines 76, 79, 100, 124
guides 49
guiding 53, 103

habituation 123
hacking 62
Ḥādīth 6, 7, 11, 20, 22, 24, 84, 90, 120
happiness 26–29
harm 120
harmonisation 42, 87
health 1, 13, 22, 39, 82, 84, 104–106, 111–115, 122, 124
Healthcare 81
hearing 40, 104, 123
heart 9, 25, 27, 30, 39, 109, 110, 117
hegemonic 12, 13, 20
hegemony 15
helping 25, 66, 110, 120
hereafter 25, 26, 28
heritage 36, 65

heroin 41
heterogeneous 103
hierarchal 7
hierarchically 25
hierarchy 110
highlighted 10
hindbrain 123
historical 7, 10, 52, 55, 65, 91
holistic 7, 9, 17, 29–31, 33, 35, 51, 85, 101
Homeostasis 123
horizontal 21, 33, 35, 45, 55, 64, 82, 85, 86, 93, 95, 98, 99, 103–106
horizontal-articulation-curriculum 105
humanism 39, 110
humanistic 30, 116, 121
humanities 21, 24, 35, 38–40, 65
humanity 4, 16, 24, 30, 40, 99
humankind 5, 26
hygiene 27
hypertension 104
hypotheses 73, 76, 79
hypothesis 51, 120

ideal 12, 51, 93, 117
identification 80, 87, 105
identify 49, 54, 57, 58, 74, 86, 87, 89, 90, 92, 94, 95, 99, 108, 111, 112, 114, 118, 121, 122
identity 10, 36, 65, 87, 120
ideological 7, 47
ideology 13, 14, 21, 49, 117
idiom 19
idiosyncratic 23
Ihsan 31
ill-health 111
illness 13, 111–113, 117
imagination 3, 29
imaginative 24, 32
Imam 2, 25, 29, 121
Imān 9
imitation 28
impartation 27
imperialism 12
implementation 18, 19, 41, 44, 61, 62, 64, 66, 68, 78, 80, 81, 88, 94, 96, 100, 103
implementing 44, 82, 87, 96
implications 8, 15, 30, 34, 44, 59, 80, 97, 124
importance 4, 15, 27, 30, 52, 53, 66, 76, 92, 101, 116
imposition 1, 36
incentive 110, 121

inclusion 11, 18, 58, 96
incongruent 43
independent 10, 12, 41, 52, 63
indicating 71, 76
indicative 79
indigenisation 15, 22
indigenous 12, 14, 15, 22, 23
individualism 36
individualistic 1, 12, 38, 118–120
individuation 120
inferential 69
infertility 113
information 46, 69, 77, 80, 82, 87, 119, 122
infusion 87
inhibit 44, 78, 97, 103
inhibitive 23
inhibitors 78
injunctions 4
innovation 44, 56, 66, 78, 81–83, 96
innovative 81
input-process-output 121
inspiration 6, 7, 28, 110
Institute 6, 21, 34, 44, 45, 61, 67, 69, 83, 97, 98, 105, 117
institutional 7, 15, 19, 36, 58, 61, 70, 81, 96, 97
instrument 67, 68, 90
integrating 2, 16, 42, 50, 61, 62, 68, 78, 82, 87, 94, 103, 105
integration 1, 2, 6–9, 12, 14–22, 24, 27–29, 31–33, 36, 37, 39, 40, 42–47, 51, 55, 61–68, 71–105, 107, 119
integrative 57, 60, 85, 98
intelligence 11, 33, 81, 108, 110, 120
intended-learning-outcomes 59
intentions 49, 52
interactions 65, 111, 113
interconnection 28
intercultural 20
interdepartmental 88
interdependence 100, 103
interdisciplinary 51, 81, 84, 86, 87, 93, 98
internalized 51
International 6, 20–22, 34, 35, 44–46, 48, 49, 59–61, 67, 80, 82, 83, 85, 94, 97, 98, 104–106, 109, 115, 117, 119
interpretation 4, 5, 34
interpretations 88
interventions 1, 9, 19, 33, 52, 54, 99, 106, 112, 113, 116, 122
interviewees 75, 77

Index

intrinsic 29, 110, 121
introspection 5
intuition 4–7, 9
investigation 62, 81
involvement 68, 123
Islām 2–4, 6–8, 23–26, 30–35, 38–40, 44, 45, 62, 64, 65, 75, 76, 79, 82, 99, 101, 110, 112, 113, 116, 120, 124
Islāmicisation 21, 38
Islāmicise 39
Islāmisation 2, 6, 14, 17, 30, 36–46, 61, 64, 89, 94, 97, 99–101, 103, 105, 106, 115, 117
Islāmising 37
Islām-psychology 64, 81
isolation 64, 87–89, 93

Jawziyyah 117
Judeo-Christian 2, 8, 64, 114
judgement 123
Judgements 35, 45
judgment 110, 121
jurisprudence 24, 29, 76, 84, 90
justice 20, 25, 31, 38
justification 51

Kalam 28, 29, 116
kaleidoscope 86
key 17, 21, 30, 43, 54, 56, 57, 67, 77, 103, 109, 111, 112, 115, 119, 122
Keynote 106
Khaldun's 119, 121
Khan 11, 21, 88, 98, 105, 122
Kifayah 38
Kingdom 59
know-how 121
knowledge 1–10, 12–34, 36–47, 49, 51–56, 61–68, 71–86, 88–110, 115, 117, 121
knowledgeable 18
knowledge-based 54
Kubler-Ross 112, 114

label 62, 63
labelling 120
landscape 91
language 2, 27, 31, 38, 39, 89, 110
lawgiver 29
leadership 36, 120
learner 25, 53, 100
learner-centred 51
learners 52, 53, 85

learning 25–29, 32, 35, 41, 45, 47–60, 62, 64, 66, 81–83, 85, 86, 92, 93, 95, 97, 100, 101, 104, 105, 107, 108, 110, 111, 114, 118, 121–123
lecturers 18, 44, 58, 61, 64–72, 74–82, 90, 96, 97
legislation 39
legitimacy 18, 31, 44, 62, 66–68, 71–73, 75, 77, 78, 80, 82, 83, 96, 97
lethargy 7
level-headed 41
liberal 23
liberation 15, 21, 38
library 20, 21, 74, 109, 119
lifelong 27, 81
lifespan 108
lifestyles 113
limitations 10–12, 50, 54, 58, 79, 88, 94, 101, 103, 110, 113, 115
linear 69, 85
linguistic 24, 28, 32
literacy 82
literature 2, 14, 32, 34, 62, 64, 66, 76–79, 99
localisation 123
logical 7, 8, 28, 55, 64, 90, 95
longitudinal 103
lordship 8
loyalties 36, 41
Luqman 110, 115

Madrasahs 36
magical 38
mainstream 10, 12, 14
maintenance 120
Majah 4, 11, 20
majorities 13
majority 6, 10, 37, 69, 75, 76
makeup 66
management 44, 65, 81, 82, 112, 113
mapping 13, 55, 90–92
marriage 110
Maslow's 110, 121
mastering 89–91
matching 31, 33, 120
materialism 15, 23, 36
materials 56, 74, 76, 78, 92, 94, 100, 109, 112, 115, 119, 122
matrix 92
meaningful 69
measurable 50, 53

measurement 10, 34, 44, 120
mechanisms 58, 64, 66, 77, 88, 90, 90–92, 96, 98, 108, 121, 122
media 26
medical 85, 87, 88, 98, 113
medicine 81, 82, 104, 113
memorisation 28, 110, 122, 123
mercy 25, 29
meta-analysis 81, 82
meta-curricular 86
metaphysics 24, 26, 65
methodological 39, 40
methodologies 16, 18, 27, 40, 45, 67, 80, 89, 90, 92, 100
Microaggressions 20, 22
micro-skills 105
midbrain 123
mind 4, 17, 19, 25, 28, 30–33, 59, 92
mind-body 111, 113, 116
misinterpretation 88
Miskawayh 116
modalities 97
model 9, 16, 17, 21, 27, 28, 30, 33, 35, 42, 45, 47, 48–51, 54, 56, 58, 59, 62–64, 70, 82, 84–90, 93, 95, 98–101, 103–106, 111, 113, 114, 120, 121
modelling 28, 110
modernisation 36, 37
momentum 2, 6, 14, 37
monocultural 1
monosemous 39
monotheism 8, 9, 21, 109
monotheistic 8
moral 7, 8, 23–28, 30–34, 42, 50, 61, 62, 67–73, 76, 80–82, 101, 110, 113, 121
morality 16, 29, 40, 80, 82
mosque 30, 37
motivation 19, 27, 66, 68, 71–73, 75–79, 83, 108, 110, 118–123
motivational 77, 123
Muhammad 6, 9, 24, 30, 34, 37, 84, 116, 117
multicultural 15, 22
multi-mode 58
multiple 4, 39, 42, 46, 53, 55, 69, 85, 86, 121, 124
Muslim-based 30
Muslim-majority 1, 11, 14, 17, 19
Muslims 6, 16–18, 24, 25, 36–38, 41, 42, 54, 65, 76, 110, 111
Mutazilites 116

mythological 38
mythology 19

Nafs 9, 65, 108, 109, 117
naqli 4, 62
narratives 14, 91, 115
national 24, 43, 59, 79, 82, 98
national-cultural 38
naturalism 12
naturalist 6
nature 6, 7, 9–11, 14, 17, 28–34, 37, 45, 48, 49, 59, 67, 85, 89, 98, 104, 108–110, 116, 120, 122
necessity 7, 48, 85
needs 1, 2, 33, 40, 55, 56, 58, 75, 89, 90, 92–94, 105, 110, 111, 123
negative 18, 44, 66–68, 70, 78, 120
neglected 7
negotiated 51
nervous 41, 109, 121, 123
neurobiological 121
neurobiology 123
neurochemical 122
neurochemistry 123
neurocognitive 120
neurodegenerative 124
neuroimaging 122, 123
neurologic 124
neurological 120, 122, 124
neuromodulators 123
neuron 109, 123
neuronal 123
neuropsychology 84, 123
neuroscience 110, 121–123
neurotransmitters 109, 123
Nexus 82
non-aggressive 120
non-discursive 54
non-integration 63
non-Muslim 33
non-specialists 66
noradrenalin 41
norepinephrine 123
novice 105
nursing 82

obedience 110, 118, 120
obesity 82, 104, 113
objectives 34, 35, 48–54, 59, 60, 62, 89, 95, 97, 107
observation 4, 88, 94, 119
obstacles 16, 17
occupation 19, 81, 84

official 74
ontological 9, 31, 32
ontology 31, 32
open-ended 51
operant 29, 110
operational 16
opiates 123
oppression 20
oppressive 10, 36
optimism 10, 112
organic 51, 124
organically 7
organisational 41, 44, 67, 78, 80, 81, 86, 87, 96, 97, 98, 101, 103
organisational-level 78
organizations 10, 82, 83
orientalists 11, 12, 14, 17, 36
oriented 91
originates 8
over-reliance 57

paradigm 1, 2, 4, 8–11, 14, 17, 21, 29, 34, 39, 40, 42–44, 52, 60, 62, 65, 89, 96, 101, 102, 113
paradigmatic 10
paradigms 22, 80
paradox 15
parallel 36, 63, 87, 104
parent-child 110
parents 27
participants 11, 67, 69, 74–79
pathway 93
patronising 13
pedagogical 14, 58, 81, 90, 121
pedagogics 14
pedagogy 1, 26
peptides 123
perennial 24
perfection 24, 28
performance 57, 82
peripheral 109, 123
permanent 31, 113
person 23, 79, 119
personal 18, 33, 49, 51, 65–67, 77, 78, 86, 94, 105, 108, 112
personhood 22
person-social 47
perspectives 12, 15–17, 21, 31, 42, 49, 59, 61, 82, 91, 106–110, 112–118, 120, 121, 123
pharmacology 98
pharmacy 81
phenomena 4, 9

phenomenologically 109
phenomenon 8, 43, 108
philosophers 31, 35, 110, 115, 116
philosophy 26, 28–35, 41, 44, 48, 49, 56, 62, 89, 101, 104, 114–116
philosophy-ontology 43
physicians 115, 116
physiological 104, 110, 113, 121, 122
pioneer 49
planners 58
planning 47, 49–51, 55, 60, 74, 86, 87, 90–92, 94, 98, 113, 122, 123
plenum 20
pluralism 36
polarisation 120
polarised 49
policies 7, 100, 101
policy 18, 37, 41, 81, 83, 92, 97, 101
political 13, 19, 20, 37, 41, 43, 47, 82
population 1, 10, 50, 79
portfolio 108, 112, 115, 119, 122
possession 25
postgraduate 1, 13, 14, 18, 20, 33, 61, 69, 75, 83, 85, 92, 94, 96, 103
post-positivism 51
postsecondary 81
practical 6, 16, 24, 28, 43, 59, 76, 79, 80, 92, 124
practices 6, 9, 11, 13, 14, 17, 19, 23, 33, 36, 38, 41, 43, 44, 51, 60, 62, 65, 74, 75, 77, 78, 80, 81, 94–96, 108, 112, 115, 119, 122
preconceptions 89
predestination 8
predictors 66, 67, 78, 82, 97
prejudice 13, 110, 118, 120
premature 10
premises 38, 39, 89, 90
prenatal 109
prerequisites 92
prescribed 43, 109, 112, 115, 119, 122
presentation 106
prevention 74, 78, 83, 111, 114
primary 4–6, 24, 74, 78, 82, 89
prime 19
principles 8, 9, 23, 24, 26, 30–34, 38–40, 42, 44, 58–60, 82, 89, 97, 99–101, 103, 105, 111, 116, 119–121
priorities 108, 112
problematic 1, 13, 38, 88
problems 10, 15, 18, 19, 24, 29, 44, 58, 68, 75, 81, 83, 88, 97, 105, 108,

109, 111, 113, 116, 117, 122, 124
problem-solving 55, 110
proceedings 24, 35, 44, 105
process 2, 3, 6, 14, 15, 19, 22, 24–27, 29, 30, 37, 38, 40–43, 45, 47–51, 54, 56–58, 61, 62, 65, 66, 68, 75, 80, 84–90, 92, 93, 95–101, 105, 109, 110, 117, 119, 124
procreation 124
produce 13, 15, 25, 26, 32, 33, 43, 47, 61, 85, 90, 92, 99
professional 14–16, 18, 33, 49, 53, 56, 59, 61, 66, 67, 69, 75, 77–79, 81, 82, 94, 96, 101, 108, 112
programmes 1, 13, 17, 19, 27, 33, 43, 47, 49, 51–59, 61–63, 85–88, 94, 99, 100, 101, 104, 105, 107, 111, 114, 118, 121
progression 87, 92, 105
prominent 10, 104
promoting 32, 51, 85, 111
promotion 51, 59, 114
propagation 14
Prophet 6, 9, 24, 29, 84, 90, 110
prophetic 104, 113
prosocial 118, 120
protocol 106
provision 26, 31, 33, 55, 67, 80, 92
pseudo-conceptual 14
psychiatric 124
psychiatry 109
psychoanalysis 116, 120
psychobabble 64
psycho-ethics 32
psychological 1, 2, 9, 12–16, 19, 20, 43, 64, 65, 82, 85, 104, 105, 108–110, 113, 116, 117, 120, 121, 123, 124
psychological-oriented 2
psychologies 22
psychologists 1, 2, 10, 11, 14, 17–20, 33, 44, 62, 64, 75, 77–79, 96, 97, 107–110, 115, 122
psychometric 81
psychomotor 50, 54, 55, 100, 105
psychoneuroimmunology 113
psychopathology 116
psychophysics 40, 122
psycho-secular 64
psychosocial 1, 9, 19, 111, 113, 117
psychosomatic 113, 117
psycho-spiritual 117
psychotherapeutic 33, 52
psychotherapist 52, 53
psychotherapists 105
psychotherapy 14, 52–54, 62, 74, 76, 78, 81, 89, 96, 105
purification 12, 22, 31
purifying 6
purpose 9, 16, 23–29, 31, 32, 37–40, 43, 57, 60, 69, 76, 85, 86, 88, 94, 107, 109, 111, 114, 118, 121
purposeful 40, 47, 49
pyramid 54, 123

Qadar 109
Qalb 9, 65, 108, 109
qualification 23, 31, 67
qualitative 67, 69, 74, 76–79, 81, 114
quality 10, 23, 33, 56, 57, 59, 60, 79, 93, 95, 101, 120, 121
quandary 18
quest 7, 28, 36
questionnaire 67–69, 71, 77, 81, 83
Qur'ān 3–9, 21, 24, 25, 27, 29, 31, 33, 63, 84, 89, 90, 104, 106, 108–110, 115, 116, 120, 122, 124
Qur'ānic 8, 104, 123, 124

race 15, 20, 21, 39
race-neutral 13
racial 20, 21, 24
racism 15, 20, 22, 36
Rahmah 48, 76
Rahman 29, 30, 35
raising 95
Ramadan 104, 124
ramifications 13
random 63, 79
randomising 63
Rassool 1, 2, 6, 8, 9, 11, 12, 14, 16–18, 21, 22, 31–33, 35, 37, 43, 45, 62–64, 76, 82, 83, 90, 95–99, 101, 103, 106, 109, 112, 115, 117, 119, 122
rational 4, 7, 24, 29–31, 38, 42, 49, 50, 62, 94, 96
rationalism 7, 8
rationalist 1, 10
rationality 1, 4, 7, 9
reactions 112–114
readiness 19, 61, 62, 66, 67, 75, 78, 80, 82, 83, 101
realisation 24

reason 1, 5, 7, 9, 32, 37, 38, 110
reassertion 41
reawakening 37
receptors 123
recessive 109
recognition 11, 25, 30, 33, 36
recommends 12, 29, 87
reconceptualised 91
reconstruct 2, 43
reconstruction 47
recreational 28
reductionism 10
refers 6, 14, 18, 38–40, 42, 57, 62, 64, 84, 104, 105
reflection 17, 28, 58, 68, 71–73, 76
reflective 49, 51, 76, 92, 108, 112, 115, 119, 122
reformation 38
reformers 37
reforming 30, 44
regression 73
regressions 69
Rehabilitation 113
reinforcement 29
rejection 17, 39
relation 6, 13, 25, 26, 56, 64, 75, 77, 82, 89, 105, 112
relationship 1, 10, 27, 29, 33, 53–55, 65–67, 76, 77, 81, 108–111, 113–115, 120, 124
relaxation 28
relegation 23
religio-cultural 14, 37
religion 1–3, 9, 10, 12, 22–24, 26, 27, 29, 30, 38, 39, 44, 75, 82, 89, 104, 108, 109, 115
religio-philosophical 15
religiosity 10, 18
religious 4, 9–11, 14, 15, 17, 20, 23, 26, 27, 29–31, 33, 37, 40–42, 76, 85, 110, 113, 116
reluctant 18, 54, 66
remembrance 3
remodelled 2
remodification 95
renaissance 7, 28
replication 121
representation 42, 79, 123
reproduction 121, 124
re-project 40
requirements 59
research 9–12, 14, 15, 21, 33, 49, 52, 59–62, 65–69, 74, 76, 79–83, 90, 100, 101, 105, 111, 113, 114, 119, 123
research-based 33
researcher 79
resistance 20, 21, 44
resolution 120
resource 76, 97
responsibility 15, 18, 27, 61, 75, 77, 95, 104
restrictive 92
restructuring 21, 35, 45, 62, 82, 98, 106
retardation 124
revealed 6, 7, 29, 39, 42, 43, 62, 71, 101, 124
revelation 1, 4–10, 12, 21, 26, 32, 37, 65
review 18, 20, 34, 44, 59, 62, 81, 82, 89, 94, 99, 106
revision 16, 59, 60, 86, 93, 95, 97
revitalisation 26
rewards 123
routes 15
rules 26

sacralised 41
sacred 39, 42, 45
sacrifice 18
Sahin-Francis 82
salience 110
salvation 26, 28
sample 10, 64, 67, 69, 70, 72, 76, 78, 79, 107
satisfaction 83
schemas 119
scheme 92, 93, 95, 107, 111, 114, 118, 121
schizophrenia 36, 124
scholars 2, 6, 7, 12, 22, 26, 29–31, 35, 37, 41, 42, 52, 64, 83, 89, 91, 96, 99, 104, 110, 114–117, 121
scholarship 17, 89, 116
schooling 50
sciences 5–7, 14, 16–18, 20, 21, 23, 24, 28–31, 33–35, 38–45, 61–63, 65, 69, 76, 81, 83–85, 89, 94, 96–98, 103, 104, 117, 121
scientific 6, 7, 10–13, 17, 21, 24, 25, 32, 39, 40, 42, 49, 89, 96, 101, 113, 123
sclerosis 124
scope 41, 45, 55, 62, 65, 68, 85, 86, 90–98, 103–105, 113
secondary 4, 83

Index 135

secular 6, 8, 10–12, 14–16, 18, 19, 22–24, 31, 36, 38, 40, 41, 43, 49, 63, 65, 94, 96, 107–110, 112, 118
secularisation 6, 10, 37
secularism 10, 23, 36, 37, 44
secularist 44
Seerah 84, 90
segment 79
segmentation 64
segmented 29
self-assessment 57
self-awareness 112
self-directed 27, 29
self-efficacy 81, 83, 113
self-esteem 66, 120
self-evaluation 58, 120
self-labelling 120
self-neglect 120
self-presentation 120
self-purification 116
self-regard 120
self-reported 67, 79
self-selected 79
self-striving 120
self-styled 41
seminar 34, 52, 59, 94
sensation 122, 123
senses 24, 31, 121, 123
sentiments 75
separation 6, 10, 37
sequencing 92, 107
sequential 87
serotonin 40, 123
sexes 124
Shari'ah 31, 33, 41, 42, 76, 89
significant 1, 10, 14, 17, 66, 67, 72, 73, 77, 89, 101
simplistic 49
sincerity 32
skeleton 55
skill-based 54
skills 18, 23, 26–28, 33, 47, 49, 53, 55, 80, 81, 86, 90, 92–96, 100, 105
Skinner 2, 17, 18, 22, 78, 83, 117
smoke 70
socialisation 23, 31
socialising 120
socio-behaviour 120
socio-cultural 2
sociology 39, 89, 119, 121
socio-moral 8
solution 89

soul 6, 9–11, 22, 25, 31, 65, 99, 104, 109, 116
soullessness 15
specialists 42, 81
spinal 123
spiritual 1, 7–9, 11, 12, 15, 17, 19, 24–27, 30, 32, 33, 37, 42, 52, 104, 107, 108, 110, 113, 116, 117, 121
spirituality 1, 2, 10, 16, 23, 25, 113, 121
split-brain 123
sprinkle 62–64, 96
stages 54, 58, 101, 103, 108–110, 112–114, 117, 118, 122, 124
standardised 73
statistical 10, 41, 58, 69
stereotypes 13, 110, 119, 120
stigma 13
strategies 20, 33, 48, 56–58, 80, 98, 101, 110, 113
stressful 86
strong 28, 52, 55, 75
structuralism 114, 116
structures 42, 44, 62, 97, 123
student 20, 27, 29, 43, 50, 52, 53, 55–58, 60, 68, 101
student-centredness 51
student-focused 52
sub-disciplines 1, 51, 84, 85, 88, 91, 94, 96, 97, 104
subject-based 87
subjectification 23, 31
subjectivity 79
sub-modalities 123
subscale 71–73, 76, 77
subservience 40
substance-using 82
Sufism 116
Sulaiman 40, 42, 45, 46
Sunan 20
Sunnah 4, 6, 8, 9, 16, 17, 31, 33, 89, 116
superiority 4
supernatural 9
supervision 81, 94
supervisors 58
support 18, 44, 47, 55, 62, 66–68, 71–74, 77–81, 92, 97, 111
supported 7, 36, 78, 92
supportive 74
supremacy 13, 14
symptoms 113, 114, 124
synchronous 84
synergistic 84

136 Index

synthesis 7, 42, 43, 47, 54, 62, 65, 84, 85, 95
systematic 47, 49, 90, 106, 114
systems 12, 14, 36, 88, 111, 123

ta'dib 24–28, 30
Tafsir 20, 28, 84, 90
Tahdhib 28
tail-end 58
tantamount 11
Taqleed 19
Taqwa 5
tarbiyah 24–26, 28, 30, 120
taṣawwur 3
Tawhîd 8, 9, 24, 29, 31, 37, 101, 102, 113
Tawhîdic 8, 62, 65
taxonomy 50, 54, 59, 60, 95, 97, 100
Tazkiyah 31
teacher 27–29, 35, 43, 45, 50, 52, 53, 55, 57, 81, 83, 87, 98, 100
teaching 1, 6, 7, 18–21, 23, 26, 27, 29, 31–33, 39, 43, 44, 47–49, 51–53, 56–62, 64, 66–70, 72, 74, 75, 77, 78, 80, 81, 83–87, 92–97, 100, 101, 104, 105, 107, 116, 121
teaching-learning 80, 100
teaching-toolkit 59
teamwork 48, 55, 76, 120
technology 58, 60, 66, 77, 81, 82, 83, 105
teleological 23
temological 43
temperament 121
temporal 37, 87, 88
temporary 113
terminal 114
terminology 26, 42, 111, 123
thematic 19, 61, 69, 74, 81, 84
theologians 29, 115–117
theological 17, 42, 52, 65
theology 11, 16, 17, 20, 22, 29, 65, 82, 96, 116
theoretical 1, 10, 15, 28, 43, 90, 99, 103, 108, 111
theoretically 79
theories 10, 12–15, 19, 26, 41, 65, 90, 107, 109, 110, 113, 118–120
therapy 11, 65, 124
three-dimensional 86
time-bound 53
time-honoured 62
top-down 18

tradition 3, 14, 17, 36, 38, 39, 42, 43, 54, 62, 89
traditional 14, 36, 38, 39, 58, 64, 85
traditionally 86
traditions 2, 6, 15–17, 22, 23, 25, 27, 37, 61, 65, 89, 91, 105
training 15, 16, 18, 24, 28, 31, 49, 58, 74–76, 78–80, 85, 93, 94, 97, 98, 105, 121
transdisciplinary 84, 87, 88, 93, 95, 104
transferability 79
transformation 21, 38, 43, 97
transmission 24, 123
treatment 113, 117
triadic 42

Ulūm 36
Ummah 6, 19, 24, 33, 37, 38
unconscious 10
undergraduate 1, 13, 14, 18, 21, 33, 49, 61, 75, 85, 92, 94, 96, 103, 105, 107
UNESCO 34, 98, 105
unholy 41
unification 84
universal 13, 24, 32, 33
universities 1, 12–14, 18, 19, 45, 64, 82
unscientific 11
unseen 6, 11, 12, 108, 110
upbringing 28
urgency 62, 97
usefulness 78
utilisation 89
utilise 44, 89

validation 19
value-added 49
values 2, 6, 7, 11, 12, 14, 18, 19, 23, 26, 28–33, 36, 37, 39, 41–43, 48–51, 55, 61–82, 84, 94, 100, 101, 105, 108, 112, 115, 121
variables 15, 66, 67, 69, 72, 76
variants 120
veneration 37
verbatim 69
verification 3
verses 3–5, 25, 63, 108, 109
vertical 21, 33, 35, 45, 55, 64, 82, 85, 86, 93, 95, 98, 99, 103–106
vertigo 123
virtues 116
virtuous 25, 121
visual 29, 123

Index   137

volition 123
volunteer 70

Wal-Jamā'ah 9
weaknesses 10, 57, 109
wealth 28
webinars 62
well-being 100
well-defined 52
well-mannered 25
wellness 111
Western-centric 12
Western-oriented 6, 37, 89
white 12–14, 20, 21
whiteness 1, 13, 21
wholesale 14
wisdom 15, 20, 25, 31, 39, 44, 110

withdraw 69
women's 112, 113
workshops 62, 74, 75, 78, 94
world 6, 9, 11–13, 20, 24, 25, 28, 31, 35,
    38, 40, 45, 64–67, 81, 83, 85,
    89, 104, 108, 114, 118, 120
worldview 7, 8–10, 12, 14, 16, 29, 31,
    32, 39, 40, 42, 43, 61, 62, 65,
    100, 101
worship 8, 9, 26, 65

Yaqeen 25
young 81
youth 20, 60
Yusuf 39, 40, 46, 116

Zarabozo 10, 12, 22

Taylor & Francis eBooks

www.taylorfrancis.com

A single destination for eBooks from Taylor & Francis with increased functionality and an improved user experience to meet the needs of our customers.

90,000+ eBooks of award-winning academic content in Humanities, Social Science, Science, Technology, Engineering, and Medical written by a global network of editors and authors.

TAYLOR & FRANCIS EBOOKS OFFERS:

A streamlined experience for our library customers

A single point of discovery for all of our eBook content

Improved search and discovery of content at both book and chapter level

REQUEST A FREE TRIAL
support@taylorfrancis.com

For Product Safety Concerns and Information please contact our EU representative GPSR@taylorandfrancis.com
Taylor & Francis Verlag GmbH, Kaufingerstraße 24, 80331 München, Germany

www.ingramcontent.com/pod-product-compliance
Lightning Source LLC
Chambersburg PA
CBHW051749230426
43670CB00012B/2218